Using the Transference in Psychotherapy

Using the Transference in Psychotherapy

William N. Goldstein, M.D.
Samuel T. Goldberg, M.D.

JASON ARONSON
Lanham • Boulder • New York • Toronto • Oxford

Published in the United States of America
by Jason Aronson
An imprint of Rowman & Littlefield Publishers, Inc.

A wholly owned subsidiary of The Rowman & Littlefield Publishing Group, Inc.
4501 Forbes Boulevard, Suite 200, Lanham, Maryland 20706
www.rowmanlittlefield.com

PO Box 317
Oxford
OX2 9RU, UK

British Library Cataloguing in Publication Information Available

Library of Congress Cataloging-in-Publication Data

Goldstein, William N.
  Using the transference in psychotherapy / William N. Goldstein, Samuel T.
Goldberg.
    p. cm.
  Includes bibliographical references and index.
  ISBN 0-7657-0341-6 (cloth : alk. paper)
  1. Transference (Psychology) 2. Countertransference (Psychology)
  3. Psychotherapy. I. Goldberg, Samuel T. II. Title.
  RC489.T73G653 2004
  616.89'14—dc22

                                                          2004004804

Printed in the United States of America

♾™ The paper used in this publication meets the minimum requirements of American
National Standard for Information Sciences—Permanence of Paper for Printed Library
Materials, ANSI/NISO Z39.48-1992.

Contents

Introduction

This book provides both a historical and a contemporary overview of the concept of transference, particularly as it relates to psychotherapy. It is written especially for students and mental health professionals at the early stages of their careers; yet it is also meant to be a useful reference for more experienced professionals.

There are two dominant themes in this book: the "old" versus the "new" models of transference, and the role of transference in psychotherapy. Regarding the former, the traditional—or classical—view of transference, termed the "old," is contrasted with a more modern relational view of transference, termed the "new." The old model views transference as a displacement of feelings and thoughts (and defenses against these) from the important people of childhood to a relatively neutral, anonymous, and abstinent therapist. Transference here is based both on the actual and fantasized past, as experienced by the patient. The new model places more emphasis on the "joint creation" of the transference by patient and therapist. Here the therapist, like the patient, is viewed as a unique individual, with his own theory of how therapy works, his own idiosyncracies, his own conflicts, his own past, and his own strengths and weaknesses, all of which contribute to the unfolding of the transference. Thus the transference is seen to be jointly constructed between the two unique individuals. Implicit in this model is that the therapist need not be, and in fact, cannot be, neutral, abstinent, and anonymous. Instead he is free to speak more openly and to participate in a more interactive and self-disclosing way. The authors approach the transference from both models, the old and the new. Both perspectives are seen to have merits. While some patients do better with the old model and others with the new, many patients do well with either model. These and related issues are elaborated throughout the book.

Regarding the theme of the role of transference in psychotherapy, this book compares two commonly used types of insight oriented psychotherapy. These two therapies are contrasted by their focus on the transference. In one, the transference is central; in the other, the transference is peripheral. The first, termed analytically oriented psychotherapy and modeled after psychoanalysis, looks to the formation and resolution of the transference as the primary therapeutic agent. The second, termed dynamically oriented psychotherapy, downplays the role of transference in this regard. Dynamically oriented psychotherapy emphasizes the formation and maintenance of a positive therapeutic or working alliance, and the use of that alliance to explore and gain understanding into the patient's conflicts without an active exploration of the transference. The difference between these two forms of psychotherapy, in addition to their applicability, is detailed in this book. These two forms of psychotherapy are seen to occur on a continuum of psychotherapy, with the most insight oriented approaches at one end of the continuum, and the most supportive approaches at the other end. This continuum, discussed in greater detail throughout this volume, includes psychoanalysis, analytically oriented psychotherapy, modified analytically oriented psychotherapy, dynamically oriented psychotherapy, and supportive psychotherapy.

As background for these dominant themes, Part I of the book provides a historical framework. Chapter 1 begins with a historical overview of transference from the old or classical perspective. It starts with the work of Sigmund Freud, then moves to a brief selective summary of important subsequent literature on transference from a classical perspective. Included here are Melanie Klein, Strachey, Sterba, Anna Freud, Fenichel, Greenacre, Stone, Arlow, Brenner, Gray, and Busch. Continuing with the historical overview of transference, Chapter 2 focuses on the new perspective. It begins with the work of Merton Gill, transitional figure between the old model and the new, then proceeds with a selective review of some of the recent literature regarding the new model. Included here are the relational movement and intersubjectivity, Hoffman, Renik, Aron, Greenberg, Stolorow, and Atwood. A section on selfobject transferences is included, as well as a look at the motivational system approach of Lichtenberg. The chapter ends with a section on the relevance of the work of Fonagy on mentalization. Chapter 3 provides a historical overview of countertransference, beginning with the work of Sigmund Freud and including the Balints, Fenichel, Annie Reich, Little, Winnicott, Heimann, Racker, Sandler, Gabbard, and Jacobs. Chapter 4 focuses on the therapeutic alliance and includes the work of Sigmund Freud, Sterba, Zetzel, Greenson, Stone, and Brenner.

Part II, "The Transference in Psychotherapy," addresses the main themes of the book, already elaborated. Chapter 5 details the old versus the new models of transference. Chapter 6 compares analytically oriented psychotherapy (with its focus on transference) to dynamically oriented psychotherapy (where the transference is regarded as peripheral). Chapter 7 details the continuum of psychotherapies already mentioned, including psychoanalysis, analytically oriented psychotherapy, modified analytically oriented psychotherapy, dynamically oriented psychotherapy, and supportive psychotherapy. The concepts of projective identification and of enactment are somewhat elusive to many. Yet, these concepts are crucial to understanding the transference according to a selected group of psychotherapists. With this in mind, Chapter 8 focuses on projective identification, enactment, and the transference.

Part III is the clinical section of the book. Here a number of detailed cases are provided, graphically demonstrating how transference is addressed and dealt with in psychotherapy. Cases demonstrate analytically oriented psychotherapy, dynamically oriented psychotherapy, and psychoanalysis. Although many of the examples are those with more classical approaches, detailed commentary on the old versus the new models is provided. Throughout this section numerous clinical items discussed in the book are demonstrated in action.

Part I

HISTORICAL OVERVIEW

Chapter One

The Old Model of Transference

One of the primary themes of this book is the current controversy between those promoting the old model of transference, based on classical psychoanalysis and originating with Freud, and those promoting the new model, based on the joint creation of the transference. This theme will be most clearly summarized from a contemporary viewpoint in Chapter 5. In this chapter, we begin our historical overview of transference with the work of Sigmund Freud. Following this, we provide a brief selective summary of important subsequent literature on transference from a classical perspective. Chapter 2 begins with Merton Gill (1979), considered a transitional figure between the old model and the new, and then proceeds with a selective summary of the literature from the perspective of the new model.

SIGMUND FREUD

It was Sigmund Freud (1917) who first recognized the phenomenon of transference. In his earliest psychoanalytic practice Freud had the expectation that, having come to a physician for help, the patient would rationally wish to cooperate with the advice of this professional, a presumably knowledgeable authority, whose expertise was offered in the spirit of detached, benign, but neutral helpfulness. Freud thought he was going about the business of helping the patient find relief from her present-day distressing symptoms through helping her understand the personal past from which those symptoms had emerged.

It was thus with some surprise that Freud found instead that he himself regularly became the focus of "quite peculiar" behavior on the part of the patient, who "began to develop a particular interest in the person of the physician." For example, the patient might become quite curious about the therapist's private life, his personal history, or his thoughts and opinions about all sort of matters. The patient might begin to express feelings and thoughts of her own about the therapist, whether critical or idealizing, angry or grateful, and might wish or expect some interaction between the two of them beyond the accustomed work of doing the therapy. The patient might "act out" (outside the therapy sessions) in order to avoid thinking about or experiencing aspects of her complex internal reactions toward the therapist. Freud (1917) called these phenomena "transference," because he believed that these were intense feelings of affection or antagonism, "which the patient had transferred onto the therapist, justified neither by the therapist's behavior or by the situation that had developed during the treatment."

Freud gradually had developed the method of "free association", which advised the patient to notice and speak openly about all his thoughts, feelings, and perceptions. The emergence of transference at first seemed a distraction from and obstacle to the primary therapeutic work of the patient: collaborating with the therapist, by using the process of free association, to understand through the emergence of memories, how the symptoms had emerged. That is, transference was seen as a "resistance" to the therapy, a resistance which Freud (1917) thought needed to be overcome by showing the patient that his feelings did not originate in the current situation, and did not really concern the person of the physician. Instead, the patient was reproducing something that had happened to him long ago.

Freud originally held a "narrow" view of transference, emphasizing a model that posited the continuing role of experiences and fantasies from childhood, and their associated urges, wishes, fears, affects, and reworkings. Scenarios, or story lines, were created that involved primary love objects from the child's early life, e.g., parents and siblings. The central organizing fantasies of these scenarios could be highly complex, in effect comprising "scripts" with many intrinsic relationship aspects.

Because it would be uncomfortable for the adult to remember or express these wishful and fearful memories/fantasies consciously, they were avoided, disguised, or "repressed," i.e., kept out of awareness. Though the now unconscious feelings, urges, and fantasies remained active, seeking expression in consciousness or behavior, the adult person's mind often disguised or displaced them into "derivatives", whose sources were not recognized. Transference represented one of these derivatives, expressing various aspects of the unconscious story lines disguised through displacement of wishes or fears onto the therapist, who was substituted for the original object, e.g., the parent.

Treatment emphasized connecting the present to the past through bringing these unconscious phenomena into consciousness. The elaboration, exploration, and working through of the transference became a prime method for accomplishing this task. The examination of unconscious urges, feelings, fantasies, memories, motives, attitudes, and perceptions in the here-and-now of the transference gave the patient a genuine new experience. This new experience provided a sense of conviction, of real meaning, relevancy, and force.

Transference thus became a vehicle or means for making the unconscious conscious. The relationship to the therapist became a key avenue for the unconscious impulses or fantasies to gain conscious awareness and expression. Freud saw transferences as "new editions" of the original "infantile neurosis" (conflictual situations, feelings, and symptoms in childhood) toward earlier significant figures, e.g., parents, now experienced toward the therapist. In other words, the patient now experienced with the therapist in the transference the same "neurotic" problems, conflicts, feelings and symptoms that she experienced toward her parents in childhood. There thus emerged a "new, artificial neurosis," the "transference neurosis," the mastery of which would coincide with undoing the core conflicts causing the very problems for which the patient originally sought help.

The transference neurosis was thought to occur when the patient's core problems were transferred onto the therapist. At this point in time the therapeutic relationship would take on heightened importance, assuming a central role in the patient's life. It was the formation (and subsequent resolution) of the transference neurosis that was viewed by some as crucial for successful psychoanalytic therapy. The transference neurosis was thought to involve and activate not only the patient's symptoms, but additionally the structure of his personality traits and character.

From Freud's classical perspective, the patient brought to each new relationship an already existing unconscious structure or script, which had had a continuous formative impact on his personality. This script would likewise have a formative impact on the new relationship in therapy, independent of the idiosyncrasies of the therapist. The patient would be predetermined to carry out this same script, regardless of who his future therapist might be. Within this model, the personality and character traits of the therapist were clearly secondary to the "internal structure" of this predetermined script in the patients mind.

With Freud, the conceptualization of transference remained narrow but changed over the years. Originally, it was seen as an unbidden phenomenon springing up in the therapeutic situation, an impediment. Later, it was acknowledged as a source of valuable information, and an inevitable and indispensable opportunity and tool of therapy. For those who believe in the classical tradition, most of Freud's ideas about transference still stand. What follows in this chapter is a brief selective overview of the important post-Freud literature, from the classical perspective.

KLEIN AND STRACHEY:
OBJECT RELATIONS AND TRANSFERENCE

Although Freud recognized that even the earliest preverbal experiences of the infant can have a significant impact upon subsequent personality development, he tended to emphasize the older, verbal child's engagement in "triangular" relationships involving not only the mother, but also the father and siblings. Correspondingly, he applied this emphasis to the transference. Melanie Klein (1952), by contrast, focused on those aspects of the transference that originated in early infancy. She elaborated theories of the infant's psychology in the first weeks and months of life, when the preverbal baby is still strongly attached to the mother dyadically. From earliest infancy on, she claimed, all mental processes—love, hate, fantasies, anxieties, and defenses—are "indivisibly linked with object relations." Therefore, "transference originates in the same processes which in the earliest stages determine object relations" (p. 436). The strength of transference feelings, and the rapidity and extremity of their fluctuations (especially in people with more severe difficulties), follow from these processes having originated in early infancy. Not only emotions, defense, and aspects of the object relations are transferred, but also the child's "total situation." Thus, the transference is a new object relationship. The patient's perceptions of and responses to present reality rest upon and are distorted by underpinnings of unresolved past conflicts that, having originated in infancy, might be quite intense and primitive.

Freud (1932) had pointed out that it is the young child's relation to his parents that originally motivates him to "be good, not bad." This lasting teaching, his moral conscience, originates as an identification with the parents' prohibitions, by which the child resolves external conflict with them and renounces forbidden wishes. There results an internalized mental structure, the superego, which thereafter stands guard within the mind, overseeing the person's thoughts and behavior, warning, encouraging, sometimes punishing, sometimes rewarding. Projection of this structure, the superego, is a commonplace transference happening in all therapy. It was James Strachey (1934), however, who focused most clearly on this phenomenon.

Working within a framework somewhat influenced by Melanie Klein, Strachey pointed out that neurotic people often suffer from internal imagos of the parents, memory distorted by fantasy, which were excessively harsh, punitive, and critical. In his real life outside of therapy, a person may by projection expect from others the same harshly punitive or condemning responses as have been meted out by his old, internal archaic imagos of authority. In extreme cases, this may create vicious cycles of conflictual aggressive interactions with other people, dominating the person's life.

The therapist, occupying a uniquely privileged position between fantasy and reality, finds himself in "the place of the patient's superego," upon whom the hostile projections are thrown and from whom they are expected back. The very absence of behavioral response from the therapist may serve to point out to the patient the distinction between his fantasy and reality. Most importantly, the therapist's verbally interpreting this transference, calmly and nonjudgmentally, makes it clear that the patient's perception of him is unrealistic, distorted by the projections. As the patient recognizes the discrepancy between these expectations of the childhood fantasy and this new real experience, he internalizes a new imago of authority, a new bit of superego. There results a gradual alteration of the quality of the patient's superego, which must be reorganized as the new bits are integrated, making it less rigid, restrictive, harshly self-critical, and unadaptable, instead permitting the patient to regard and treat himself more as the therapist has—tolerantly, respectfully, calmly, and kindly. Quite importantly, Strachey held that it is the interpretation of these episodes in the here-and-now, at the point of urgency, where the forbidden impulses, feelings, and wishes toward the therapist are active and emotionally immediate, that more than any other factor has mutative effect, i.e., helps the patient achieve lasting change.

STERBA, A. FREUD, AND FENICHEL: EGO, DEFENSE ANALYSIS, AND TRANSFERENCE

Richard Sterba (1940) described a therapeutic separation effected within the patient, between an experiencing and a self-observing ego. In interpreting the transference, the therapist implicitly invites the patient to identify with his calmly observing mental functioning, rational, curious, reality-oriented. It is these same healthy and mature potentialities in the patient that are facilitated and nurtured by the identification. The observing ego of the patient becomes a strong ally with the therapist.

Sigmund Freud had thought that therapy should aim primarily to recover awareness of the memories, fantasies, and impulses that have been kept disguised and unconscious by the defenses. Anna Freud (1936), by contrast, emphasized that what may be most observable and most accessible to therapeutic intervention is not the transference of the original libidinal and aggressive impulses, but instead the transference of the defenses which had been set up against them. What made Anna Freud's work revolutionary was her grasping that the patient's defenses are just as important an aspect of his personality as the aspects that are more deeply unconscious. The fact that the defenses, although themselves generally unconscious, are more closely allied with the person's conscious image of himself makes them potentially more easily accessible to influence.

With regard to addressing the defenses, the critical distinction between what will be helpful or counterproductive for the therapy seems to lie in the therapist's attitude. If the therapist conveys to the patient that he regards a defense as an obstacle, in the way, a distraction, or as uncooperativeness, and seeks to circumvent or attack it, he will seem in effect to be telling the patient that he's been bad, and will not be respecting the patient's need for the defense. The patient will most likely feel threatened, in that what for years he's relied on for safety (the motive for the defense to begin with) is being undermined; he may simply increase his resistance, and the therapist will be in the position of one who, in trying to untie a knot, merely pulls it tighter. Instead the therapist must accept the patient's need for the defense and use patience, tact, and sensitivity in his approach. Conveying to the patient that the therapist is not interested only in what is repressed and frightening, but also in the patient's attitudes toward what he finds unacceptable within himself, helps the patient feel that he is accepted and respected fully, as a whole person.

Otto Fenichel (1941), following Anna Freud, recommended that one start "from the surface, down," and address the defense before what is defended. This may require a gradual process of first acknowledging how the patient views his situation. In time, one isolates a defense and demonstrates it to the patient clearly. Then, one might raise tactful questions about it to stimulate the patient's curiosity about himself. The mere nonjudgmental observation of a defense often serves to undermine it, so that material representing what it was defending against often then begins to emerge spontaneously. Over time, the therapist can help the patient see that the defense has seemed necessary in order to diminish unpleasant feelings associated with some memory or fantasy the patient would rather not think about. Ultimately, the therapy might lead to the patient's recalling how that defense originated historically, and also to his understanding of why it has been necessary to employ it in the therapy, e.g., in relation to some perception, fantasy, or feeling regarding the therapist.

Otto Fenichel also pointed out that the responses of all people in every interpersonal situation always involve a mix, both of elements appropriate to the external reality and also of subjective elements from within, transferred from the past. What makes the therapeutic situation unique is that the therapist's nonintrusive neutrality influences the patient as little as possible, so that the transference elements of the patient's responses can be seen most clearly.

GREENACRE AND STONE:
BASIC, PRIMORDIAL VS. MATURE TRANSFERENCE

Phyllis Greenacre (1954) considered the "basic transference" or "primary transference" to derive from a "primitive social instinct", intrinsic to human nature, for each individual first manifested and engaged in "the original infant-mother quasi-union" (p. 672). The patient, needing help, develops "an attitude of expectant, dependent receptiveness" toward the therapist, expressed to some degree in basic trust in the therapist's integrity and competence to help. This concept dovetails with that of Freud's (1912) "unobjectionable positive transference." As with Sterba's ideas regarding the observing ego, it relates to the therapeutic or working alliance, to be elaborated in Chapter 4.

This basic transference raises the question of how to avoid engendering dependency and instead promote the patient's maximal ultimate autonomy. Greenacre thought that this goal was best promoted by the therapist remaining neutral and abstinent—not overtly guiding or suggesting, leaving decisions up to the patient about how he should conduct his life.

Leo Stone (1967) acknowledged that the wish to achieve a bodily reunion with mother, at least symbolically, is normal and ubiquitous, though largely prohibited and repressed. He questioned, though, whether in therapy such an early situation of infant-mother quasi-union is actually reproduced. Moving in an opposite direction, he defined a "'primordial transference'"—as derived from the effort to master, and from longing to undo "a series of separations from the mother."

In contrast to the primordial transference, Stone defined the mature transference as "the wish to understand and to be understood; the wish to be given understanding . . . the wish to be taught 'controls' in a nonpunitive way" (p. 24). He also included "the wish to be seen in terms of one's developmental potentialities," (ibid.), and the wish to do well in collaborating in successful therapeutic work. Stone noted that, in the therapeutic dialogue, the patient's speaking freely and the therapist's interpreting can be seen as echoing the dialogue between a young child and mother. Just as the child takes pleasure in asking questions of and learning from the parent, so also there is a legitimate gratification, "functional pleasure," in gaining from the therapist ever greater clarity and understanding, psychological-mindedness, and maturity. While the primordial transference awakens longings to return to an infantile relationship with the parent, the mature transference tends toward greater autonomy, separation, and individuation, and promotes a more "neutralized" relationship with the original objects.

ARLOW, BRENNER, AND BUSCH: MODERN STRUCTURAL THEORY AND TRANSFERENCE

Already implicit in many of the descriptions of transference, starting with Freud, was a conceptualization emphasized and brought into sharpest focus by Arlow and Brenner. (1964; Brenner 1982). We have already seen that transference combines reality with fantasy, past with present, conscious with unconscious, and that it serves many functions simultaneously, both expressive and avoidant. For Arlow and Brenner, transference, like every other mental experience and behavior, simultaneously expresses all the functions or forces of the mind, which inevitably conflict with one another. The synthetic, integrative tendency inherent to the mind tentatively or stably resolves the conflicting interests by forming a compromise. Transference, then, represents one such compromise solution to conflict. We therefore expect to find explicitly or implicitly in every transference both love and aggression, drive expression and defense against drive expression, moral ideal and prohibition, reward and punishment, and perceptive adaptation to reality side by side with efforts to avoid the challenges of reality.

Concepts such as Arlow and Brenner's are often subsumed under the rubric structural theory, because all the structures of the mind, the mental apparatus, are seen at all times to participate in all mental functioning, as can be witnessed most directly and fully in transference. Paul Gray (1994) and Fred Busch (1999), drawing heavily on Anna Freud, focus on the patient's mind as a fluid process that can be observed and addressed in the transference moment by moment.

Gray and Busch demonstrate emerging drive derivations and defensive shifts that occur in the here-and-now of the therapy hours. By paying close attention to the patient's flow of associations, staying close to the surface, and always aware of the projection of the role of authority onto the therapist, Gray and Busch demonstrate conflict as it occurs in the here-and-now. They do this in a rather systematic way, in a manner that pays close attention to the patient's observing ego and to his sensitivities and vulnerabilities. They feel that this method diminishes the role of the therapist as an authority and gradually enables the patient to expand his conscious ego.

Chapter Two

The New Model of Transference

In this chapter we continue our historical overview of transference. We begin with Merton Gill (1979, 1982), considered a transitional figure between the old model of transference and the new, the latter emphasizing the joint creation of the transference and summarized in Chapter 5. We then proceed to selectively review some of the recent literature regarding the new model. This chapter includes a section on selfobject transferences and on related work of Peter Fonagy regarding mentalization.

MERTON GILL

"Transference and resistance inevitably follow from the fact that the analytic situation is interpersonal." (Gill 1979, p. 263) To a generation of psychotherapists who had conceptualized psychotherapy as focusing on the psychology of "one-person", i.e., aiming to discover, understand and influence the structure of the mind within the patient, this statement by Merton Gill may have seemed new and provocative. In the twenty-plus years since his landmark paper (1979), however, many authors have widened psychotherapeutic observation and conceptualization to a more interpersonal, intersubjective, two-person psychology. Gill's work challenged the classical view by which transference was conceived as derived from repressed memories, urges, fantasies, and the defenses against them, originating primarily in relation to key figures in the person's past. Instead, Gill emphasized that transference included the patient's natural, spontaneous responses to the present situation, in which the therapist was a new, present, real object, whom the patient to some extent (consciously or unconsciously) perceived realistically.

Gill was a unique figure in the transition from the old to the new models of transference. Originating within the mainstream of classical psychoanalysis, he is responsible for one of the most quoted definitions of psychoanalysis (1954): as a therapeutic technique, employed by a neutral analyst, that permits and results in the development of an intense regressive transference, with the ultimate resolution of the transference by interpretation alone. Yet, by 1979, Gill was viewing the transference as being jointly created between analyst and therapist in the here-and-now. Originally advocating his methods for patients in psychoanalysis, he later (1982) believed that these same techniques should be applied to all therapy that focused on the transference, regardless of the frequency of sessions.

Gill's technical ideas about dealing with the transference follow his theoretical beliefs. Rather than merely helping the patient realize that thoughts and feelings about the therapist were displacements from earlier relationships, Gill believed that the transference could and should be explored and resolved through the examination and interpretation of the patient's thoughts, perceptions, and feelings as they occurred directly about the therapist, here-and-now in the office. The focus of interventions should be primarily about the present; memories of the past would follow naturally. Whatever the patient is thinking or talking about on the surface, his or her associations inevitably, pervasively, and continuously are determined at least in part by his awareness of the therapist, from the very beginning and throughout the treatment. Whether he knows it or not, the patient is always commenting about the relationship between himself and the only other person in the room.

In working with the transference, Gill distinguished two forms of interpretation. For a considerable time, the therapist should interpret "resistance to awareness of the transference." Only later, after the patient has become conscious of feelings and thoughts centering on the therapist, would it be possible to interpret "resistance to the resolution of the transference" (p. 264). In resistance to the awareness of the transference, the transference itself is what is being resisted. Rather than expressing thoughts, fantasies, and feelings about the therapist directly, the patient may do so indirectly, displacing them into disguised allusions, perhaps about persons or situations in his life outside the therapy, there-and-then. To overcome this tendency, the therapist would aim to help the patient see that these indirect allusions may plausibly refer to latent thoughts and feelings about the therapist, here-and-now. Likewise, the therapist may interpret the patient's acting out as an unconscious defensive means of avoiding awareness of transference feelings emerging in or stimulated by the therapy. There thus results a movement of the work of the therapy from discussion of the patient's outside difficulties, to discussion of the patient's conflicts within the transference in the here-and-now.

Gill thus elucidated the principle that all transference has a connection with something in the present, actual therapeutic situation, which provides the necessary medium for the expression of the transference. Therapeutic focus would start with actual experiences and interactions in the here-and-now. As mentioned, some would say that Gill moved therapy from a one-person toward a two-person psychology, in which the most relevant "unit of observation" was less the dynamics of the patient's intrapsychic structure, and more the patient-therapist dyad. With Strachey, Gill believed that therapeutic interventions that are most likely to be ultimately mutative, i.e., causing lasting change, are transference interpretations in the here-and-now.

Following Gill, various authors have carried his challenge further, claiming that it is impossible for the therapist to be purely neutral, objective, abstinent, or uninvolved. Rather, inevitably, the therapist is also unconsciously striving to manage his own conflicts over unacceptable wishes, feelings, and fantasies, also in part derived from his own personal past. The therapist inevitably has countertransference to the patient, which contributes to the development of their relationship as much as does the patient's transference to the therapist. Rather than seeing the transference as a preset program from the past within the patient, "brought to" and imposed upon the treatment, this new view argues that the two people as external objects for one another cannot help but mutually affect each other in the present. Transference and countertransference intimately, subtly, and unconsciously respond to one another and develop together. This perspective thus sees the therapeutic relationship as a new joint creation.

THE RELATIONAL MOVEMENT AND INTERSUBJECTIVITY

Although proponents of this new model of transference come from all schools of thought, the modern originators are predominantly from the relational movement and the school of intersubjectivity. The relational movement was spearheaded by Greenberg and Mitchell (1983) in the early 1980s, basically as a reaction to classical psychoanalytic thinking. Although contemporary in origin, this movement can actually be traced back to Ferenczi (1932), who is credited with initiating the first important shift from Freud's method. Today there is overlap between relational theory, intersubjectivity, and social constructionism. Intersubjectivity, although more associated with self psychology, is quite similar to the relational school in regard to the transference. Social constructionism, originated by Irwin Hoffman (1983), has basically been incorporated within the relational movement. In all of these schools, the psychotherapeutic experience is thought to be an intersubjective one, in which the transference is thought to be jointly created by patient and therapist. Emphasis is on co-participation, mutuality, and new experience between patient and therapist. De-emphasis is on anonymity, abstinence, and neutrality. Psychotherapy is thought to unfold in accordance with a commingling of transference and countertransference. With this brief overview, we will sample only a few voices and ideas amongst many on this rapidly progressing frontier.

Irwin Hoffman (1983), originally writing in conjunction with Gill, is responsible for the term the joint construction of the transference. As noted, he is the originator of the school of social constructionism, referring to the joint *construction* of the transference in a *social* interactive framework (Natterson and Friedman 1995). Hoffman (1996) is additionally known for his focus on dialectics. Important dialectics regarding the transference include the dialectic between the therapist as an authority and the therapist as a person like the patient. Additionally, there is the dialectic between the repetition of old experiences (related to the old model of transference) and the construction of new experience (reminiscent of the new model of transference). For Hoffman, the free emergence of multiple transference-countertransference scenarios replaces that of free association as a central focus of attention, authenticity and spontaneity are emphasized, and neutrality is deemed as impossible.

Owen Renik (1999), trained as a classical psychoanalyst, but adopted by the relational movement, emphasizes the ongoing role of the therapist's subjectivity within the psychotherapy process. The therapist's individual psychology, his past, his personality, and his countertransference, all play a continuing essential role. With this in mind, Renik believes there is continual countertransference enactment within the psychotherapy process. (See Chapter 8 for more on enactment.) As with Hoffman, transference-countertransference intermingling provides the raw material of technique.

Lewis Aron (1991, 1996), working within a similar framework to that of Hoffman and Renik, also emphasizes the continual intersubjective experience between patient and therapist. Believing the process to be mutual, although asymmetrical, he focuses special attention on the subjectivity of the therapist. With this in mind, Aron recommends asking the patient to speculate about what the therapist might think or feel, or even about what the therapist's internal conflicts might be. Aron believes that this overt focus on the subjectivity of the therapist enables the patient to focus analogously on people outside of the psychotherapy situation.

Jay Greenberg (1986, 2001), elaborating in a similar vein, emphasizes the patient's continuous influence on the therapist in addition to the myths of neutrality, abstinence, and anonymity. He offers a novel new definition of neutrality, based on a relational perspective. Neutrality here is viewed as an optional tension between the patient's tendency to see the therapist as an old object (related to the old model of transference) and the patient's capacity to experience him as a new object (akin to the new model of transference). Greenberg believes that both are needed for successful therapy.

As noted, similar concepts to those of the relational school have been introduced by the school of intersubjectivity, spearheaded by Stolorow and Atwood (Atwood & Stolorow, 1984; Stolorow, Brandschaft, & Atwood 1987). Proponents of this school speak of intersubjectivity (and mutual influence) whenever two people are together, regardless of their developmental level. In contrast, many of the relational group (Benjamin 1990; Stern 1985) view subjectivity more as a developmental landmark. With this in mind, Benjamin (1990) does not speak of subjectivity until the child is able to conceptualize the other (the mother) as a person with her own needs and desires, separate from the child. Here Benjamin differentiates the mother as an object whose sole purpose is to meet the child's needs from the mother as a subject with her own distinct needs and desires. These concepts, of course, apply to the transference in psychotherapy.

SELFOBJECT TRANSFERENCES

No review of transference is complete without the inclusion of the selfobject transferences. Although not emphasized in this book, these transferences are clearly relevant and important in all psychotherapy. Self psychology began when Kohut (1971, 1977, 1984), working within the framework of classical psychoanalysis, described the spontaneous emergence of one of several elaborately described transferences—the mirror, the idealizing, and the twinship—during the course of psychoanalysis. These transferences are the original selfobject transferences.

In self psychology, a selfobject is considered to be a function, not a person (Wolf 1988). However, selfobject experiences are typically brought about by people. In fact, most of the earliest selfobject experiences are in relation to people. These people provide functions necessary to maintain the more dependent individual's psychological integrity. Initially people providing the selfobject function are experienced as part of the self; later in life they can be experienced as separate.

Self psychology emphasizes the importance of selfobject experience from birth till death. These experiences are needed to provide necessary self cohesion and self esteem. They additionally provide enhancing experiences such as soothing, comforting, strengthening, validation, and vitality. Selfobject needs are ubiquitous, occurring in all relationships. In psychotherapy they appear as selfobject transferences. These selfobject transferences are thought to operate overtly in the foreground or silently in the background. In these transferences the therapist is experienced as a function that helps maintain and organize the individual's sense of self (Lachmann 2000), providing a source of self coherence, affect regulation, self-continuity, self-enhancement, and self-restoration.

As noted, Kohut initially described three types of selfobject transferences. In the mirroring transference, the patient's needs to be affirmed, recognized, confirmed, and appreciated, are met by the selfobject. In the idealizing transference, the patient is able to experience herself as being part of an adored, respected, powerful, and protective selfobject. In the twinship, the patient experiences an essential likeness to the selfobject. Others (Wolf 1988) have described additional selfobject transferences. In the adversarial transference the patient experiences the selfobject as a benignly opposing force, who is supportive and responsive while allowing and encouraging an oppositional stance. In the merger transference, the patient experiences herself to be one with the selfobject. In the efficacy transference, the patient experiences himself as having an impact on the selfobject.

Selfobject needs were originally differentiated from object needs. In object needs, the other person was viewed as an autonomous and independent individual. In selfobject needs, the other person was viewed as someone providing needed functions (Baker and Baker 1987). Lachmann (2000), in regarding transference, designates a selfobject dimension and a representational dimension. The selfobject dimension includes the experience and maintenance of the tie to the therapist, who provides the selfobject functions already noted, such as cohesion, vitality, and self esteem. The representational dimension, the dimension emphasized in this book, refers to the qualities of the self and other, including the themes of that relationship. Both dimensions are always in the transference, either in the foreground or in the background. Selfobject experiences and selfobject transferences are not emphasized in this book. This lack does not mean that we do not value these concepts. In fact, we feel that the selfobject dimension of transference plays an important and vital role in all psychotherapies.

MOTIVATIONAL SYSTEMS

A contemporary subgroup of self psychology, the motivational system approach of Joseph Lichtenberg and his colleagues (Lichtenberg 1989; Lichtenberg, Lachmann, & Fosshage 1992, 1996) emphasizes five motivational systems within the context of infant and child research and an intersubjective framework. The five motivational systems—regulation of physiological requirements, attachment/affiliation, exploration/assertion, aversion, and sensual/sexual enjoyment—function to develop and maintain the cohesiveness of the self or self organization. Within this model, the transference is conceptualized in accordance with which of these motivational systems is currently operative (in the foreground).

PETER FONAGY

These days no review is complete without reference to Peter Fonagy and his work on mentalization (1991; Fonagy et al. 1993). Fonagy's concept of mentalization actually is similar to Benjamin's (1990) concept of the mother as a subject. The term mentalize is used by Fonagy to mean the capacity to conceive of conscious and unconscious mental states in oneself and others (Fonagy 1991). For the child to learn to mentalize, Fonagy (Target and Fonagy 1996) believes that there must be an early intersubjective relationship between the child and the parent (or significant other) where the parent behaves toward the child in a way that helps her to understand her own behavior (and that of others) in terms of ideas, beliefs, feelings, and wishes.

Fonagy (Fonagy et al. 1993) relates his ideas of mentalization to the transference by elaborating two schematic models that highlight the psychotherapy process: the representational model and the mental process model. In the representational model, via the transference, there is a rearrangement and reorganization of mental representations. This model is consistent with a number of others regarding therapeutic change. By contrast, the mental process model is used in cases where a whole class of mental representations appears to be absent from the patient's functioning. Correspondingly, there is the absence of the capacity to mentalize. In this model the therapist plays a role analogous to the parent of a small child in helping the patient to develop the capacity to mentalize.

Chapter Three

Countertransference

Traditionally, transference and countertransference were considered separate, distinct, although very related phenomena. Today they are often viewed as intertwined, intermingled, blurred, and in fact inseparable. This latter view is certainly that of those promoting the new model of transference but it is also subscribed to by some proportions of the old. With this in mind, we will elaborate this essential concept in this chapter.

Freud (1910) coined the term countertransference in 1910 as follows: "We have become aware of the 'countertransference', which arises in the physician as a result of the patient's influence on his unconscious feelings. . . . No psychoanalyst goes further than his own complexes and internal resistances permit; and we consequently require that he shall begin his activity with a self-analysis and continually carry it deeper." This narrow definition of countertransference refers to these unconscious reactions of the therapist to the patient, which, causing blind spots, impede his therapeutic functioning. More recently, Kernberg (1984) offered an even more restricted, but commonly applied, definition as the therapist's "unconscious reaction to the patient's transference."

Countertransference was at first viewed as episodic, only a part, one aspect, of the therapist's total attitude toward the patient. Moreover, as it involved unconscious, disguised, irrational, and emotional mental functioning in the therapist—indicating perhaps some conflicts not fully resolved in his own personal therapy—countertransference was viewed as problematic, analogous to a symptom. Its emergence seemed antithetical to the purposeful, rational, reality-oriented professionalism required of the therapist. As sometimes did actually occur, countertransference was thought generally to present dangers of imposing upon, contaminating, and interfering with the work of therapy.

A wide definition of countertransference, by contrast, includes all the thoughts, reactions, and feelings that the therapist has toward the patient, both conscious and unconscious. This includes the therapist's responses not merely to the patient's specific transferences, but to the patient as a whole, including her character traits, physical appearance, demeanor, employment, and external life circumstances. The therapist's own character traits and attitudes, as well as his own ethno-cultural, socio-economic, and gender identifications, with their implicit, possibly unnoticed biases, all contribute to determining the therapist's thoughts, perceptions, attitudes, and reactions toward the patient. Moreover, life circumstances and events for the therapist outside of his work, such as concerns about professional prestige or family worries, might well impact his perceptions of and reactions to the patient. Douglas Orr (1954) wondered if the term countertransference should ". . . comprise everything the [therapist] brings to the [therapeutic] situation—his office, his technique, and all that he was, is, and ever hopes to be" (p. 658).

Today countertransference is portrayed as ubiquitous and inevitable. The therapist's entire subjectivity, conscious and unconscious, is thought by some inevitably to be both affected by and affecting the patient and his transference. Almost everyone now agrees that, however it is defined, countertransference provides, not an obstacle, but an invaluable source of information about what is going on both within the patient and between the two participants in the therapeutic dyad.

HISTORICAL OVERVIEW TO 1954

As the literature on countertransference is vast, our historical overview will only provide a few highlights. As early as 1939, Balint and Balint (1939) pointed out that, far from being a completely blank screen that does not impinge on the patient, the therapist impacts in countless ways beyond his technical clarifications and interpretations. The therapist's manner of dress and demeanor, his style of speech, affective responses, ways of dealing with scheduling and billing, all affect the patient and presumably the transference. The Balints nevertheless held that patients "are able to adapt themselves to most of these individual atmospheres and to proceed with their own transference, almost undisturbed by the [therapist's] countertransference" (p. 94). By contrast, many modern writers argue that the patient's transference is in large part a direct response to the therapist's countertransference. This is at the heart of the new model of transference.

Countertransference as dysfunction was emphasized by Fenichel (1941) who warned that the therapist in countertransference is "making use of the patient" for some piece of "acting out" determined by the therapist's past, seeking gratification of unconscious wishes in the relationship. In a similar vein, Annie Reich (1951) wrote that countertransference consists in "the effects of the [therapist's] own unconscious needs and conflicts on his understanding or technique. In such cases, the patient represents for the [therapist] an object of the past onto whom past feelings and wishes are projected" (p. 26). It is thus exactly analogous to the process of a patient's transference onto the therapist. Acting out occurs when the activity of doing therapy has unconscious meanings for the therapist. "Then, his response to the patient, sometimes his whole handling of the [therapeutic] situation, will be motivated by hidden unconscious tendencies. . . . Some needs of the [therapist], such as to allay anxiety or to master guilt feelings, are gratified." Little (1951) pointed out that, insofar as countertransference is a specific and repressed "transference" to the patient, it is a compromise formation, synthesizing both aggressive and libidinal gratifications and prohibitions. That is, the countertransference, structured like any symptom or character trait, follows the "principle of multiple determination," and serves many simultaneous functions. Thus, the therapist may be largely responding not to the reality but to his fantasy about the patient.

On the other hand, Winnicott (1947) pointed to the "truly objective countertransference, . . . the [therapist's] love and hate in reaction to the actual personality and behavior of the patient, based on objective observation" (p. 195). Beyond the observation of the patient as someone external, the inner subjectivity of the therapist can also be regarded as objective data. Using the contemporary metaphor of a telephone receiver, Freud (1912a) had described the "remarkable fact" that the unconscious of one person can communicate with the unconscious of the other. According to his recommendation for "free-floating attention," the therapist consciously should hover between listening to and observing the patient's verbal and behavioral productions, while also introspectively noticing all of his own thoughts, feelings, daydreams, and associations. Their apparently spontaneous, involuntary production in the mind of the therapist in fact occurs by unconscious processes partially in response to the patient. For Heimann (1950), the reaction of the therapist may be the first useful clue to what is going on in the patient. The therapist's unconscious resonates with and provides unconscious understanding of the patient, a "rapport on the deep level," which leads to an emotional response that can guide the therapist's cognitive understanding.

HEIMRICH RACKER

Because of the importance of his contributions, we will present the thoughts of Heimrich Racker (1957, 1968) in somewhat greater detail. Racker showed

in detail how countertransference reactions "may be used as tools" to illumi-
nate with subtlety and richness the psychology of the patient. He emphasized
that strong countertransference emotions may be not only normal and nonpathological, but inevitable. Relying on Kleinian concepts, he demonstrated
how both participants are linked by the same psychological processes operating in each. The participation of each continuously affects the experience of
the other.

Quite interestingly, Racker, in his famous article in 1957, saw the patient's transference as containing his fantasies about the therapist's countertransference. This would follow from a definition of transference-fan-
tasy as involving an interpersonal script or scenario in which both people
actively participate and have experiences. We might extrapolate that the
therapist's countertransference includes his fantasies about the patient's
transference.

Regarding countertransference, Racker differentiated between what he
called concordant identifications and complementary identifications, both
of which the therapist makes with the patient. He spoke in terms of object
relations theory, where various pairings of internal self and object representations, derived from both actual past experience with significant others
and also from fantasy, compose each person's internal psychic structure. In
a concordant identification, the therapist identifies with and feels sympathy
for the self-experience of the patient; that is, he identifies with the patient's
self-representation. This form of empathy often is allied with what has been
called the "positive countertransference". In a complementary identification, the therapist identifies with the patient's corresponding internal object;
that is, he identifies with the patient's object representation.

For example, a patient may have a partial self-image as a bad child expressing frustration angrily, paired with an internal image of a scolding or for-
bidding parent telling the child to keep quiet and threatening punishment. Experiencing and presenting himself as the humiliated bad child, he may
unconsciously project the accusing parental attitude onto the therapist. If the
therapist accepts that projection and identifies with the patient's denied critical attitude toward himself, he would be manifesting a complementary countertransference. If, on the other hand, the therapist feelingly reassures the patient, he would be manifesting a concordant countertransference.

Suppose the therapist has unresolved conflicts toward a particular aspect of
his own personality. For example, because of fears of his own passivity, he
might unconsciously reject passive feelings within himself and defend against
them with exaggerated assertiveness. He then may be unable to identify with
a patient's conscious but conflictual passivity. That is, he will have decreased
a concordant countertransference. The therapist instead may be more likely to

identify with the patient's self-condemning attitude toward his passivity, and exhibit a complementary countertransference.

Of key importance is whether the therapist is conscious of experiencing certain thoughts and feelings in relation to the patient, as a "minimal neutralized" reaction, or a "trial identification" (Reich 1960). If so, he will better be able to maintain distance, recognize the experience as alien to his self, stay somewhat objective, and make use of the information to guide his interventions. A very self-aware therapist may be able consciously to recognize, accept, and contain even what would be socially unacceptable thoughts and feelings, "his own infantile object relations with the patient." Such conscious tolerance and reflection in the therapist allows him to escape reenacting the patient's original pathogenic conflictual experience, whether real or imagined, and instead permits interpretation, which interrupts the vicious cycle and opens up new possibilities of experience and understanding for the patient.

As opposed to this, a therapist who remains unaware of the effects of countertransference may find his self-experience overcome with the identifications (or with what the patient projects), so that he loses objective distance. His strong feelings may be mistakenly rationalized as justifiable. The experience becomes too real, and rather than being a participant-observer, he becomes an actor in the drama. If protracted, this could develop into what might be termed a countertransference neurosis. It is then that the vicious cycle for the patient may be perpetuated, the therapy becoming a mere repetition of what he experienced and enacted throughout his life, without the distinguishing features that make therapy uniquely useful.

To illustrate: A therapist may imagine some thoughts or feelings about herself, in a particular context, which she hopes not to hear from the patient, because they would bring up painful feelings or self-doubts. Noticing this within herself can serve as a clue to what the patient may be not expressing. That is, the patient may be subliminally aware of what would be too upsetting for the therapist to hear, and would be defending himself against the discomfort associated with this correct fantasy by not mentioning it, while at the same time protecting the therapist from pain that he anticipates causing. The therapist might then inquire if the patient is keeping from noticing any thoughts he may be having about her. We can thus see the "relation between a transference resistance and a countertransference resistance." We might extend Racker's conclusion to note how the intrapsychic dynamics within each, each secretly wishing and fearing, each defending privately against some painful fantasy or feeling, interact in such a manner as to constitute a mutual, dynamic field of reciprocal coparticipation.

JOSEPH SANDLER

Joseph Sandler (1976) posited that any person's core wishes and mental processes "are expressed intrapsychically in [descriptively] unconscious images or fantasies, in which both self and object in interaction have come to be represented in particular roles." (p. 46) In ordinary interpersonal life, especially when object-seeking, a person unconsciously attempts to impose an interaction, prods or manipulates, in order to provide a specific role response from the person with whom he is dealing. This target may either refuse to accept the role or may accept it and act accordingly. Thus also, a patient in therapy naturally "attempts to actualize these [roles] in a disguised way" thereby resisting becoming aware of their infantile roots.

Sandler broadened Freud's concept of free-floating attention to also include the therapist's behavioral reactions: "free-floating responsiveness". He thus also in effect was broadening the understanding of countertransference, as a normal process within the therapist inevitably affected by the patient. The concept now would encompass not only thoughts, feelings, and fantasies, that might be unconscious or consciously experienced, but also seemingly spontaneous behaviors, whether grossly obvious, or quite subtle. Role responsiveness thus segues into the concept of enactment.

Sandler sees the therapist's responses, experienced and expressed, as "a compromise formation between his own tendencies and reflexive acceptance of the role which the patient is forcing on him." It would be therefore inaccurate either to see the therapist's response as strictly an indicator of what's going on within the patient, or to see it as strictly a result of the therapist's own intrapsychic pathology. In his free-floating responsiveness, the therapist will "tend to comply with the role demanded of him . . . [but] may only become aware of it from observing his own . . . responses . . . after these have been carried into action." The process involves a reciprocal exchange of complex unconscious cues.

GLENN GABBARD

In his review of the literature since about 1950, Glenn Gabbard (1995) saw therapists from different theoretical orientations arriving at a common understanding of countertransference through integration of the concepts of projective identification and enactment. Because of their importance, Chapter 8 will be exclusively devoted to further exploring these two concepts. Projective identification, a term originally introduced by Melanie Klein, has been conceptualized by later writers as an interpersonal process, by which a person disavows an intolerable aspect of himself (a partial self-image, feeling, attitude, or impulse) and projects it into the other person, for example, a therapist. In a manner often so subtle as to be difficult to recognize as it happens, and thus sometimes quite confounding to the therapist, the patient behaviorally, consciously and/or unconsciously, applies coercive pressure for the therapist to experience or unknowingly identify with what has been projected. The recipient or target of the projection, if unaware of what is occurring, may then very well experience and enact the projected role as Sandler (1976) described. Gabbard feels "that the capacity for the therapist to 'participate' in a projective identification may depend upon there being some 'hook' in the recipient of the projection to make it stick." The hook may consist in the therapist's pre-existing unresolved conflicts, or, what may amount to the same thing, in the susceptibility or valency for the reactivation of aspects of the therapist's self-representation. The therapist's countertransference is thus a "joint creation by both patient and analyst."

TED JACOBS

As Ted Jacobs (1997) has summarized, the so-called analytic instrument refers to the mind of the therapist focused upon the patient in a particular way. The data of the therapist's inner experiences can be taken as informing the therapist about the patient's psychological experience and expressions, only if the therapist has given himself over totally to the patient and has entered a unique state of mind which allows him to resonate with the inner life of the patient. There then can emerge in effect a unified instrument between the two unconscious minds of the patient and therapist resonating, each thus permitting the emergence between them of sensory stimuli, memories, and fantasies, as well as physiological responses and enactments. This unified instrument, so conceived, clearly is constituted of nothing but the patient's transference and the therapist's countertransference, intimately and reciprocally responding, each to the other. Harry Smith (2000) has claimed that it forms a unified transference-countertransference structure.

Jacobs cites recent work showing that a child obtains his view of his own inner world by way of the fantasies of the parents or caretakers, which "play a central role in structuring the infant's psychic reality." (1997, p. 1049) Analogously, it is possible that in therapy, patients change not only through cognitive insight into their conflicts from interpretations, but also "via the incorporation of aspects of the [therapist's] perceptions, both conscious and unconscious, of the patient's psychic reality." (ibid) Consider the vast amount of data, not only the complex, detailed historical life narrative, but also the direct interpersonal experience lived and observed with the patient, that a therapist over time must integrate. The therapist deeply involved in his work may well develop a fantasy or vision, largely unconsciously synthesized, of what kind of person this human being might become, and what kind of life he could possibly live. This countertransference also may be implicitly communicated by the therapist and subliminally picked up by the patient, who through this silent exchange may thus form new identifications, and internally conceive for himself larger possibilities and broader horizons.

In summation, countertransference today has attained equal status with transference both theoretically and practically, as a source of essential data both for understanding and for intervention. The therapist is seen as merely human, affected, subjective, and fallible, equally with the patient. His own unconscious memories, feelings, fantasies, impulses, and scripts are drawn in and implicated continuously in his functioning as "therapist," in the formation of the patient's transference, and in the interpersonal developments between them, the therapeutic relationship as "a new creation."

Chapter Four

The Therapeutic Alliance

Another of the primary themes of this book is the differentiation of two commonly used forms of dynamically based psychotherapies, one where the formation and the resolution of the transference is seen as the primary therapeutic agent, and a second, where the transference is deemed as peripheral. The former is labeled analytically oriented psychotherapy, and the latter dynamically oriented psychotherapy. Dynamically oriented psychotherapy emphasizes the formation and the maintenance of a positive therapeutic alliance as a crucial ingredient. With this in mind, we will focus on the therapeutic alliance in this chapter. Chapter 6 will provide a summary of the similarities and differences between analytically and dynamically oriented psychotherapy.

We begin with a paragraph briefly and simplistically differentiating the therapeutic alliance from the transference. For our purposes in this paragraph, the therapeutic alliance and working alliance are identical, and are included in the real relationship. These concepts are related to the observing ego (Sterba 1940) and the basic or primary transference (Greenacre 1954), already described. All these ideas originated with Freud's (1912) idea of the unobjectionable positive transference. The concept of transference here will readily be recognized as that of the old model.

The therapeutic alliance is the collaborative relationship between patient and therapist, established to facilitate the work of psychotherapy. It demands that the patient maintain an observing ego that continually focuses on the therapeutic process. This observing ego is in alliance with the therapist against the patient's conflicts and resistances. Although it can include unconscious components, the therapeutic alliance operates mainly on a conscious level. In contrast, the transference is an unconscious process, in which the patient displaces or transfers onto the therapist feelings and thoughts that were originally directed toward the important people of early childhood. The transference includes not only these feelings and thoughts, but also defenses against them. It is based on both the actual and fantasized past, as experienced by the patient.

As will be rapidly seen, the distinction between the therapeutic alliance and the transference is not always so obvious. In actuality there is much overlap, and it may be impossible to completely separate the two concepts.

Important figures in the history of the concept of the alliance include Zetzel (1956), responsible for the term therapeutic alliance, and Greenson (1965), responsible for the term working alliance. Zetzel pointed out that the relationship with the therapist was not only a transference relationship, but also a new, real situation for the patient, presenting real demands in the present. She specified that a degree of mature mental functioning, existing before the treatment, was necessary for a sound therapeutic alliance, upon which the hope for effective treatment depended. This mature area of the personality, reality-based, autonomous, conflict-free, and therefore not needing treatment, or perhaps beyond its influence, might be taken to be separate from transference.

Greenson (1965), like Zetzel, also separated off as not transference the working alliance, the relatively non-neurotic rational rapport which the patient has with his therapist. It is reasonable, purposeful, involving motivation to overcome the patient's illness, and capability to participate in the therapeutic work. It involves realistically adaptive, rationally observing functions, including the ability to assess both oneself, the therapist, and also the relationship from a distance. The working alliance is relatively "neutralized," neither sexualized nor angry.

Greenson felt that by the time the [neurotic] patient entered therapy, he already had the capacities to form object relationships, to tolerate frustrations, and to put off gratifications. He was thought to be capable of realistic hope, some ability to trust, to communicate verbally, to get in touch with feelings, yet to be able to restrain action. He was also able to not only split off observing from experiencing functions of the mind, but also to separate "a reasonable object relationship to the therapist from the more regressive transference reactions." Leo Stone (1967) also held to the separation of the working alliance or "real relationship" from that of transference.

Others, however, would debate this. Perhaps the patient's responses to the present situation, his readiness (or difficulty) in cooperating with the therapist, should also be included within the term transference. Indeed, this was clearly implied by Freud (1912) when he distinguished the erotic and negative components of transference from that "which is admissible to consciousness and unobjectionable (the positive unobjectionable transference) and is the vehicle of success" for the treatment. Freud felt that the patient's positive transference, connecting the therapist with the loving, kind figures in the patient's past, was required as the only force strong enough to overcome the usual resistance of therapy. The therapeutic alliance relied upon a loving attachment to the therapist, but this attachment had roots, i.e., relied on transferred feelings, imagos, and wishes, which may have been the source of the patient's problems to begin with. Though not at first Freud's recommendation, the patient's mature adult, nonneurotic relationship with the therapist, depending on stable patterns of character and consciously accepted "integrating identifications" might also become subject for investigation in the therapy.

Brenner (1979), in particular, disapproved of distinguishing between the transference and therapeutic alliance. He warned that a therapist who thought in terms of a patient misusing the therapeutic procedure could fall into merely exhorting him to behave differently or to try harder. A further risk inherent in the concept of the therapeutic alliance is that the therapist might aim to modify his own behavior instead of questioning why the patient reacts as he does. That is, the therapist might not strive to understand the patient as fully and correctly as possible. By contrast, Brenner argued that the therapist who conceives the patient's behavior less as manifesting a faulty alliance, but instead as resistance determined by unconscious conflictual transference feelings, would aim to help the patient recognize specifically how he is defending, against what, and why. If progress can be achieved, interpretation of what are the patient's conflicts, concerns, wishes, and fears will produce the same beneficial effects on the atmosphere of the relationship as will simply acting "more human," but interpretation has the advantage of also advancing the patient's self-understanding.

Stone (1967), as noted, disagreed, stating that it was best to conceptualize the working alliance, i.e., the real relationship, as not the same as the positive transference. Yet, he noted that the working alliance includes certain elements of the mature transference consciously acceptable to the patient, and also of the positive transference, which after all may motivate the patient to want to listen to the therapist, to learn and grow, to be good, to win the therapist's approval. The therapeutic alliance also includes "tender aspects of the erotic transference," adult friendly feelings, the realistically perceived need for help, and the appraisal of the therapist as competent and trustworthy.

One problem is how to distinguish a rational realistic working alliance, relying upon functions in the patient that presumably are autonomous and conflict-free, from positive transference, which needs to be understood for its hidden motives toward defense against or gratification of unconscious wishes. For example, a patient may wish to ingratiate himself, to impress the therapist, to please him, to seduce him, to be like him, to keep him interested or attached, in order to assure himself against abandonment by the therapist, or to protect himself from the therapist's disappointment, criticism, or attack. The patient may even, in a friendly way, compete with the therapist in a contest over who will be quicker at understanding. All of these cooperative, helpful attitudes may be seen to promote good work, yet also are themselves transferences derived from conflict, the components of which could become entrenched resistances. Greenson pointed out, for example, that a patient's behavior toward the therapist may be rigidly reasonable, teasingly or spitefully cooperative. He acknowledged that "the working alliance [could become] the facade for the transference neurosis."

The question arises as to how to proceed when there are problems with the therapeutic alliance. We already have noted Brenner's ideas about the need for understanding and interpretation. Greenson (1965) feels that with many, there is little to do except wait. The working alliance develops almost imperceptibly, "relatively silently," with the therapist having to do little that is special or extra to promote it. As Freud (1912) said, merely showing consistently attentive and serious sympathetic understanding will usually lead a patient "of himself" to form a friendly attachment to the therapist. Also implicit in Freud's description are the necessary attitudes in the therapist of being matter-of-fact but noncritical, calm, implicitly warm, accepting, patient, conveying hopeful expectation that their work will help the patient to grow and achieve his goals. The patient becomes an "ally" of the therapist in their work.

As Sterba (1940) described in a similar vein, the therapist, through his objectively observing and understanding interpretive functions, engages these same functions within the patient. He asks the patient to notice and wonder about his feelings, thoughts, and attitudes. With phrases such as, "We might notice . . . ," he points out similarities, parallels, connections, discrepancies, avoidances, and distortions, and raises questions, such as "Where do you think this might come from?" Greenson (1965) wrote, "The therapist's intervention separates the working attitudes from the neurotic transference phenomena." In a metaphor, we might think of the working alliance as the attempt of two diplomats to establish a calm, rational, meeting of minds for deliberation, above the fray, while their respective nations are involved in complex, perhaps intense conflict. In cases of greater difficulty, Greenson believed that the therapist may need to be more active, to show the patient what he's supposed to do, that is, how to associate freely in a way that is helpful and meaningful.

For some patients, however, such an alliance and progress does not come easily. Many borderline individuals (Meissner 1988; Goldstein 1996) present obvious problems in forming and maintaining a therapeutic alliance. This poses a major difficulty in the therapeutic work, one that needs to be focused on repetitively and continuously. Some feel that with some of these patients, it is only near the end of the therapy that the alliance becomes reasonable and workable.

With many borderline individuals the alliance is typically fragile and tenuous initially, becoming increasingly stronger gradually and incrementally with much regression and progression. In accordance with Greenson's ideas, the alliance is strengthened as the patient experiences the therapist over time as being stable, competent, consistent, conscientious, and concerned. Under the influence of these factors, the therapeutic alliance automatically develops without active intervention.

However, whenever there is any disruption in the alliance, the therapist needs to actively intervene. He needs to point out to the patient that there is a problem with the working alliance, and to invite him to explore this difficulty. Disruptions in the alliance need to be addressed, repetitively, throughout the therapy, whenever they occur.

Typical of many borderline patients is a gradual improvement in the alliance, with much waxing and waning. Thus there is often an oscillation between focus on the therapeutic alliance and focus on interventions involving other core difficulties. Unending sequences often occur as follows. Focus on the therapeutic alliance after a disruption is followed by a strengthening of the alliance, leading to a therapeutic intervention involving a core difficulty. The latter intervention causes another disruption in the alliance, and the above sequence repeats itself. As the therapy progresses and the alliance becomes increasingly stable, there is more focus on the other core difficulties and less focus on the alliance.

Part II

THE TRANSFERENCE IN PSYCHOTHERAPY

Chapter Five

Transference: The Old vs. The New

This chapter offers a contemporary view of transference. Drawing from past chapters, it looks at the traditional (or classical) view of the transference, termed the *old*, and compares it to a more modern view (based on the joint creation of the transference), termed the *new*. The proposed contemporary view looks at the transference from both perspectives: the old and the new. Both models are seen to have merits. While some patients do better with the old model and others with the new, many patients could do well with either model. These and related issues will be elaborated following a more detailed discussion of the two models.

Classically, transference has been considered an unconscious process in which the patient displaces or transfers onto the therapist feelings and thoughts originally directed toward the important people of childhood. Transference includes not only these feelings and thoughts but also defenses against them. It is based on both the actual and fantasized past, as experienced by the patient. The patient's pathological and nonpathological personality traits, as well as his symptoms, based on intrapsychic conflict, are activated in the psychotherapeutic process and become an integral part of the transference. It is the establishment and working through of the transference that is thought to be crucial to the attainment of insight in psychoanalysis and psychoanalytic psychotherapy. Traditionally, the therapist strove to serve as blank screen, in an atmosphere of neutrality, abstinence, and anonymity, thus providing a setting most conducive to the displacement of feelings.

The above is the traditional or classical view of transference, termed the old. It comes from an ego psychological perspective, but with adjustments in terminology, it can serve other models as well. Thus personality traits and symptoms need not only be thought of in terms of intrapsychic conflict.

They can be conceptualized in other ways, such as resulting from defects, from interpersonal interactions, or from lacks in parental attunement. Likewise, if one desires, the concept of defense can be altered or eliminated. In fact, whenever terms from ego psychology are used in this chapter, they can be changed, in accordance with other alternative schools of thought, if one so desires.

Implicit in the old model, whether viewed from an ego psychological perspective or not, is that transference arises in its purest form when there is little interaction between patient and therapist. Regarding the unfolding of the transference, the less the therapist is known, the better. Concomitantly, as long as the therapist remains unknown, a pure transference will emerge, regardless of the personality and character traits of the therapist. These ideas relate to the concepts of neutrality, abstinence, and anonymity.

Abstinence simply means that the therapist abstains, or holds himself back, from revealing himself. Anonymity means staying anonymous or unknown. Neutrality is a little more complicated. Technical neutrality (Anna Freud 1936) refers to the therapist's position of equidistance from the id, ego, superego, and external reality. To put this another way, it means that the therapist does not side with any of those four structures in his thinking or interventions. Instead, he maintains an attitude of free-floating attention, so that he can listen (and intervene) with equal respect, distance, and objectivity to aspects of the patient's id, ego, superego, and external reality. Although easier said than done, the use of this definition of neutrality probably would have few opponents. It is the connotation of neutrality that evokes a therapist who is distant, cold, unempathic, noncaring, and noninteractive, to which many object. Those promoting the concept of neutrality argue that one can be neutral, warm, empathic, and caring, all at the same time.

A useful modern concept of neutrality (Goldstein 2001) posits a neutral therapist as one who is nonintrusive and who steers clear of judgment and criticism. He uses the therapy sessions to carefully listen to and understand the patient, and to make interventions based on this listening and understanding. No matter how interactive he might be, he emphasizes and maintains this aim. Interventions focus on the patient, her problems and her life. In most cases the therapist, before intervening, thinks about how his interventions will influence the patient. There will be times, however, when the therapist reacts spontaneously and/or emotionally. These times are not only impossible to avoid, but can contribute usefully to the process. However, even here, the therapist uses his reactions to understand the patient. Over-identification and excessive intrusion of the therapist's life into the sessions are avoided. Neutrality as defined here is certainly compatible with a position of warmth, empathy, and concern. With the possible exception of this modern definition of neutrality (which can relate to both the old and the new), the above is the essence of the classical or traditional view of the transference: the old. Influenced initially by Gill (1979) and more recently by Hoffman (1983, 1986), Aron (1996), the intersubjectivists (Stolorow, Brandschaft, and Atwood 1987) and others, there is a recent shift in psychoanalysis and analytically oriented psychotherapy away from the blank screen model of neutrality, abstinence, and anonymity, to a process that is more interactional, interpersonal, and subjective in nature, characterized by a mingling of transference and countertransference between patient and therapist. This is the model of the new. Whereas the old model is largely subscribed to by ego psychologists, the new model is generally followed by therapists of the relational school, the intersubjectivists, and the social constructionists. Many self psychologists and a number of modern ego psychologists also embrace this model.

In the new model, the therapist, like the patient, is viewed as a unique individual, with his own theory of how therapy works, his own idiosyncracies, his own conflicts, his own past, and his own strengths and weaknesses, all of which contribute to the unfolding of the transference. Thus the transference is seen as a joint creation between two individuals, both with their own unique personalities, values, and subjectivities. From this perspective, the therapist is similar to the patient, and his authority is diminished. However, because of his knowledge and experience regarding psychotherapy, some authority is retained. Some (Hoffman 1996) see a dialectic between the therapist as an authority and the therapist as a person similar to the patient. Others (Aron 1996) view the relationship between therapist and patient in this regard as mutual but asymmetrical. With the subjectivity of the therapist thus emphasized, many now view the neutral therapist (in the old sense) as a theoretical ideal, impossible to attain in actuality. Correspondingly, the roles of abstinence and anonymity are likewise diminished.

As noted, with the emphasis on the similarities of the patient and therapist, with both having transferences that enter into the picture, the distinction between transference and countertransference becomes blurred. Thus one can think of a mingling of transference and countertransference, both of patient and therapist. Within this context, the concept of enactment becomes more relevant. (Enactment, together with projective identification, and their relation to transference, will be discussed in Chapter 8.)

Implicit in this new model is that the therapist need not be, in fact, cannot be neutral (in the old sense), abstinent, and anonymous. Some (Hoffman 1996; Renik 1996) feel that this discovery frees the therapist to speak his mind more freely, to offer more about himself, and to participate in a more interactive and self disclosing way. Of course, the more open, interactive, and self disclosing the therapist becomes, the more the blurring between the transference of the patient and the transference of the therapist. The same applies to countertransference. There is a wide range of opinion amongst therapists favoring the new model, about how interactive the therapist might be. One can postulate a continuum here, with the relative traditionalists on one end, and the "anything goes" therapists on the other. The relative traditionalists recognize the impossibility of total neutrality, abstinence, and anonymity. Yet, with some belief in the thinking of the old model, they attempt to approximate this unattainable stance as much as possible. Thus they remain relatively neutral, abstinent, and anonymous. The anything goes therapists interact and self disclose freely, without worrying about their effect on the transference. They believe that an atmosphere that emphasizes interaction provides the best framework for the patient to feel comfortable, safe, and secure, influencing her to talk freely, deeply, and without constraint. Additionally, they believe that maximum interaction does not detract from the patient's ability to transfer from the past. In other words, no matter how much the therapist relates, he will not stop the patient from transferring from the past.

Regarding therapy that promotes interaction, the question of self disclosures comes into play. Focus here is on intentional disclosures, because in all therapies there are numerous unintentional and unconscious self disclosures. The office setting, the appearance and dress of the therapist, the way he relates to the patient (including affect, animation, choice of words, accent, style and frequency of interventions), his manifest personality, his preferred theoretical model, the countertransference, plus many other factors, offer unending sources of information about the therapist. These sources of information can be considered unintentional self disclosures. Additionally there are unconscious slips or acts by the therapist. It is the ubiquity of these unintentional and unconscious self disclosures that leads some (Aron 1996; Renik 1996) to question why therapists are so cautious about self disclosures.

Regarding intentional self disclosures, there are many types. Renik (1999), for example, routinely advocates a type of self disclosure that involves the therapist revealing his thinking (sometimes in detail) about interventions he makes to the patient. Relational therapists frequently encourage a focus by the patient on the therapist's subjectivity, with selective self disclosures as part of this process. Many therapies include disclosures of quasi-personal information, including such items as the therapist's vacation plans, his marital status, his hobbies, plus political and other opinions he might hold. Psychotherapy sometimes includes some informal chit-chat about mutual interests, such as restaurants, sports, or finances. On occasion direct advice is given to selected patients.

The question remains about whether these intentional self disclosures are useful in psychotherapy that emphasizes the transference. To put this question another way, one can ask whether intentional self disclosures inhibit or contribute to the intensification and resolution of the transference, with ultimate therapeutic gain. Those against self disclosures believe that these both inhibit and distort that process. Those in favor believe that selective self disclosures help establish a comfortable and safe milieu, enhancing the patient's ability to speak easily and openly, ultimately enhancing the therapeutic process.

A crucial question that needs more exploration is whether the transference unfolds and is resolved better within the stance of the old model versus within the stance of the new model. This question is not unlike the one of whether intentional self disclosures inhibit or enhance the unfolding and resolution of the transference. Those favoring the old model feel that for the purest transference to develop, the therapist needs to be as neutral, abstinent, and anonymous as possible. Those favoring the new model feel equally strongly that interaction and reasonable self disclosure provide a better forum for dealing with the transferences. Advocates of both models present very good arguments in their favor.

The contemporary view presented here looks at the transference from both perspectives. This view maintains that both models have merits. Some patients will do better with the old model, while others will do better with the new model. Many (possibly a majority) will do well with either model. This last idea needs to be taken seriously, especially amongst those who enthusiastically recommend one perspective while devaluing the other. Of relevance here are the many patients who value their own therapies no matter what the model, insisting that the model used for them is the ideal. How many of these patients would say the same had their therapist used a different model?

A neglected point is that a set is established in the therapy in accordance with the model used. Patients identify with the particular set, become used to it, and accept it. Thus a patient accustomed to the old model might have no difficulty with her therapist's refusal to answer questions. Identifying with the therapeutic position that not answering questions will ultimately lead to better things (despite some frustration), she will staunchly support that practice. However, if a therapist using the new model typically answers questions and then refuses to do so, his patient might become quite upset. Likewise, a patient accustomed to the old model might become angry when her therapist occasionally self discloses. Correspondingly, a patient of the new model might become equally annoyed when her therapist fails to self disclose. This underlooked area of the set of the therapy, with the corresponding expectations of both patient and therapist, needs to be taken into account.

The preceding paragraphs might give the impression that the question of the old vs. the new model is a discrete issue. This impression is not necessarily the case. A better way to approach this topic is to consider a continuum

Chapter Five

perspective, with the old and new models at opposite ends of the continuum. A specific therapy can fall anywhere on the continuum. Likewise, the point on the continuum can shift within the same therapy.

Another relevant factor is the training and personality of the therapist. Some therapists do better with the old model, while others do better with the new. Additionally, some therapists are flexible enough to offer different models for different patients and to shift models if advantageous.

Thus, the contemporary view presented here maintains that both perspectives, the old and the new, have merits. While some patients do better with one perspective and others do better with the other, many patients do well with either model. The exact same things can be said about psychotherapists. Some do better with the old model, while others do better with the new. Likewise, some therapists can shift models with relative ease, in accordance with their patients' needs, and others cannot. One needs to consider a continuum model, with the old on one end and the new on the other, rather than to think in terms of discrete modalities.

Chapter Six

The Transference in Psychotherapy

This chapter discusses the role of transference in the dynamically based psychotherapies. Dynamically based psychotherapy refers to psychotherapy in which understanding (of psychodynamics) plays a central role. The original dynamic psychotherapy is psychoanalysis; all other dynamically based psychotherapies are thought to be derivatives of psychoanalysis. These therapies can be thought to occur on a continuum, with the most insight oriented approaches at one end, and the most supportive approaches at the other end. This continuum includes psychoanalysis, analytically oriented psychotherapy, modified analytically oriented psychotherapy, dynamically oriented psychotherapy, and supportive psychotherapy. This continuum will be detailed in Chapter 7. This chapter will focus on the similarities and differences between the two most commonly used insight oriented modalities (outside of psychoanalysis proper): analytically oriented psychotherapy and dynamically oriented psychotherapy. These therapies are contrasted by their focus on the transference. In one, the transference is central; in the other, the transference is peripheral. Analytically oriented psychotherapy looks to the formation and resolution of the transference as the primary therapeutic agent, whereas dynamically oriented psychotherapy downplays the transference in this regard. Here the distinctions between the old and the new models of transference, as detailed in Chapter 5, become secondary. The primary question is how much emphasis is placed on the transference.

Before describing these two types of psychotherapy, two caveats are in order. First, although psychotherapy that relies on transference and psychotherapy that does not are routinely differentiated, the terms analytically oriented psychotherapy and dynamically oriented psychotherapy are not typically used to make this distinction. Rather, these two terms are often used interchangeably.

This book, however, will differentiate the two types of therapy by the designated terms: analytically oriented psychotherapy and dynamically oriented psychotherapy. Second, practically speaking, any given therapy can be a combination of the two types. Likewise, a given therapy can switch from one predominant type to another. For whatever reason, analytically oriented psychotherapy appears to be a bit idealized and overemphasized in a number of circles, whereas dynamically oriented psychotherapy is under-acknowledged. We believe that a number of therapists who claim to be doing analytically oriented psychotherapy are actually doing psychotherapy that is predominantly dynamically oriented.

In analytically oriented psychotherapy, the therapist attempts to do therapy in a way that most simulates psychoanalysis. (For further differentiation of analytically oriented psychotherapy from psychoanalysis, see Chapter 7.) With the underlying assumption that permanent change is best effected when the patient reexperiences and works through his conflicts with the therapist, one attempts to maximize the development and resolution of the transference. Using techniques analogous to those of psychoanalysis, with an emphasis on insight oriented (versus supportive) interventions, the therapist tries to obtain an intense transference. Initially he comments on resistances to the formation of the transference; later he helps the patient to understand himself by correlating the transference with both current and childhood relationships. Differences from psychoanalysis include the frequency of sessions, the use of the chair versus the couch, and possibly the downplaying of free association. Psychoanalytically oriented psychotherapy works best with patients who are easily able to form an intense transference in the psychotherapy situation.

The trappings of analytically oriented psychotherapy involve regularly scheduled sessions, usually two but sometimes three a week, held for varying periods of time. As in psychoanalysis, there is basically no contact between patient and psychotherapist outside of the appointments. Sessions are typically conducted with the patient and therapist sitting across from each other in comfortable chairs. The patient is usually told that the sessions are hers, that she can talk about whatever she chooses. In addition to discussing topics of her choice, the patient is encouraged to report seemingly extraneous thoughts and fantasies that occur to her during the sessions. As in psychoanalysis, areas of typical resistance to such discussion are often mentioned.

Dynamically oriented psychotherapy, in contrast, emphasizes the formation and maintenance of a positive therapeutic or working alliance, and the use of that alliance to explore and gain understanding into the patient's conflicts. Focus is on present-day events and their correlation to the past. Patient and therapist together try to understand the patient's present-day interactions and relationships on the basis of her or his sensitivities, vulnerabilities, and distortions, which originate in the early years. This approach downplays the transference as a therapeutic modality. Although transference reactions are noted, especially when they occur as resistances, the elaboration and resolution of the transference does not play a major role. A positive therapeutic alliance is fostered, and the therapist is sometimes mildly idealized. Occasional suggestion and education are employed, along with insight oriented interpretations, although the former techniques are by no means emphasized.

The main difference between dynamically oriented psychotherapy and analytically oriented psychotherapy is the downplaying of the transference as a therapeutic modality in the former. This form of therapy is particularly useful with patients who cannot form a reasonably intense transference within the psychotherapy situation. It is also used sometimes with patients who easily form very intense transferences, with tendencies for destructive acting-out and disruptive fragmentation.

It is important to note that when we speak of the downplaying of the transference in dynamically oriented psychotherapy, we are specifically referring to the object-related aspect of transference. This aspect was designated as the representational dimension by Lachmann (2000) in Chapter 2 and differentiated from the selfobject dimension. The selfobject dimension is often clearly manifest in dynamically oriented work, providing needed validation, self cohesion, comforting and soothing, and other selfobject needs.

The trappings of dynamically oriented psychotherapy involve regularly scheduled sessions, usually one or two times a week, held for varying periods of time. There is little contact between patient and psychotherapist outside of the appointments. Sessions are always conducted with the patient and therapist sitting across from each other. Basically the same instructions are given to the patient as in analytically oriented psychotherapy, although sometimes the instruction to report seemingly extraneous material is omitted.

Regarding the choice of analytically oriented psychotherapy versus dynamically oriented psychotherapy, there are two major questions to consider. The first is how easily the patient is able to develop an intense transference within the psychotherapy sessions. One can only do analytically oriented work, of course, if this development is maximized. The second question is whether the patient can utilize the intense transference for therapeutic understanding and gain. Patients who can use the transference in this constructive way are contrasted to those for whom the development of an intense transference can lead to destructive acting-out and/or unnecessary fragmentation.

The next question is which patients do better with analytically oriented psychotherapy and which do better with a dynamically oriented approach. This gets into the question of diagnosis. The remainder of this chapter will briefly address this question. Although diagnosis is frowned upon by some psychodynamically oriented therapists, we find a diagnostic system that focuses on large groupings quite useful when considering psychotherapy. This diagnostic system places patients into one of four large groupings: normal-neurotic, narcissistic, borderline, and psychotic. Each of these groupings is differentiated by a focus on ego functioning. Although not currently in vogue, a focus on ego functioning is a most effective way of both describing and understanding patients. Ego functions that are used to differentiate the four large groupings include reality testing, sense of reality, adaptation to reality, thought processes, impulse control and frustration tolerance, object relations, interpersonal relations, defensive functioning, autonomous functions, the synthetic-integrative function, identity, sense of self, self cohesion, and others. These ego functions have been originally detailed by Beres (1956), Bellak (1970), and Bellak and Myers (1975). The differentiation of the four large diagnostic groupings by ego functioning has been elaborated elsewhere (Goldstein 2001) and will be summarized most succinctly here.

The normal-neurotic grouping is characterized by rather good ego functioning across the board. Despite this positive, specific difficulties in interpersonal and object relations and the exaggerated use of certain defensive patterns present problems for some individuals in this grouping. By contrast, the psychotic grouping presents the most problems with ego functioning. This grouping is characterized by specific problems in reality testing in addition to low ego functioning in general. Despite these tendencies, some individuals in this grouping can show good ego functioning in selected areas.

The borderline patient (Goldstein 1985, 1996) presents with a pattern of relative ego strengths superficially, but with underlying ego weaknesses. Because the relative strengths stand out on the surface and the weaknesses are often not obviously apparent, individuals in this grouping often look neurotic. The relative ego strengths include reality testing, thought processes, interpersonal relations, and adaptation to reality. Under stress or close scrutiny, these relative strengths can break down or be seen as superficial. Underlying weaknesses include poor impulse control and frustration tolerance, the tendency to use certain primitive defenses, major problems in identity, and marked fluctuations in affect.

The narcissistic grouping presents the most difficulty with diagnosis. Similar in a number of ways to borderline patients, narcissistic individuals differ from typical borderline patients by having a more stable sense of self and a tendency for more specific problems regarding impulsivity and affectivity. Sense of self, although cohesive and stable, is based on a grandiose identity. Regarding impulsivity and affectivity, narcissistic individuals can be especially vulnerable to perceived slights and rejections with ensuing uncomfortable feeling states (such as rage, embarrassment, shame, and humiliation) and subsequent acting-out. This is in contrast to typical borderline patients, where the problems are more global. In general, ego functioning in the narcissistic group is a bit higher than in the usual borderline individual.

Regarding this diagnostic system, many erroneously think that patients in the normal-neurotic group are ideal candidates for analytically oriented psychotherapy. To the contrary, many patients in this grouping actually have a difficult time forming an intense transference outside of psychoanalysis per se. If an intense transference cannot be formed, analytically oriented psychotherapy is not the preferred modality. With this factor in mind, many therapists favor a dynamically oriented strategy for this group if psychoanalysis itself cannot be utilized. Other therapists, however, make all efforts to utilize an analytically oriented approach. Still others employ a transference oriented strategy for those neurotics who seem easily able to form intense transferences (often hysterical in personality type), while favoring a nontransference oriented approach for those less able to do so (often obsessive in personality type).

Because borderline patients characteristically form very intense transferences quite rapidly, even without the use of the couch, the opportunity to use analytically oriented psychotherapy is clear. However, because of ego weaknesses and the propensity for too much regression, modifications in technique with the analytically oriented strategy (as compared with the approach for more neurotic patients) are usually necessary. Modifications for these patients include three areas: the therapist's neutrality, the transference, and the use of insight oriented versus supportive interventions. For details regarding these modifications, see the next chapter. With these modifications, analytically oriented psychotherapy is the preferred treatment for most borderline patients. Dynamically oriented psychotherapy is found useful by some psychotherapists for borderline patients who form transferences so intense that dangerous acting-out and destructive behaviors (related to the intense transference) are difficult to control. With some borderline patients there can be a flow back and forth from analytically oriented to dynamically oriented modalities.

Dynamically oriented psychotherapy is also found useful for a number of psychotic patients, but for many a more supportive approach is needed. Supportive therapy is especially useful for those psychotic patients with active and acute problems in a number of their ego functions. Details regarding this type of therapy are found in the next chapter. Regarding narcissistic patients, an analytically oriented psychotherapy, if not psychoanalysis proper, is often the treatment of choice. For some narcissistic patients, however, an intense transference does not evolve, and a more dynamically oriented modality is preferable.

This chapter has emphasized analytically oriented psychotherapy and dynamically oriented psychotherapy as two distinct modalities, indicated for different patients. In actuality, psychotherapy can combine these two modalities in any way. Additionally, within the same psychotherapy, there can be changes from predominantly analytically oriented to predominantly dynamically oriented, and vice versa.

At the beginning of a psychotherapy, even when the diagnostic grouping is clear, one often does not know whether the therapy will follow a predominantly analytically oriented or dynamically oriented model. Thus a good strategy for initiating psychotherapy is to have as few preconceived ideas a possible, allowing the transference to unfold and selecting interventions in accordance with this unfolding. The initial stance is one of exploration and clarification; deviations from this are in accordance with occurrences within the therapy hours. This initial strategy is conducive for the emergence of an intense transference. Time will tell whether the transference will emerge with sufficient intensity so that the therapy will be primarily analytically oriented, or if the therapy will unfold in a more dynamically oriented way.

Chapter Seven

Psychoanalysis and the Continuum of Psychotherapies

This chapter will present a continuum of the dynamically oriented psychotherapies, from the most insight oriented at one end of the continuum, to the most supportive approaches at the other end. Psychoanalysis stands at the insight oriented end. As all the dynamic therapies are derived from psychoanalysis, the chapter starts with a detailed focus on that modality. The continuum of psychotherapies to be presented includes psychoanalysis, analytically oriented psychotherapy, modified analytically oriented psychotherapy, dynamically oriented psychotherapy, and supportive psychotherapy. In this chapter there will be some unavoidable overlap with the content of the previous chapter.

Throughout this chapter reference will be made to insight oriented vs. supportive interventions. A few words about these techniques are in order. The interventions of clarification, confrontation, and interpretation are the ones most associated with insight oriented work. Briefly, clarification (Bibring 1954) means to see things in a clearer way. It refers to matters that are conscious or subconscious but not unconscious. Clarification helps the patient to become clearer about feelings, attitudes, thoughts, behavior patterns, and perceptions. The therapist often uses clarification to help the patient bring together contradictory attitudes, behavior, and ideas. Confrontation is a subgroup of clarification (Meissner 1980). Clarification usually appears more neutral on the part of the therapist, whereas confrontation involves a more intrusive stance. Confrontations are sometimes designed to create conflict where there previously had been none. Interpretation (Bibring 1954) strictly deals with unconscious material. It can refer to both defenses and that which is defended against. It often provides an explanation or a hypothesis about conscious behavior. Interpretations are often preceded by numerous clarifications.

Supportive interventions include suggestion, therapeutic manipulation, abreaction, advice, reassurance, education, limit setting, reality testing, and encouragement and praise. Unlike clarification, confrontation, and interpretation, these interventions, if used with any frequency, are more typical of supportive work.

PSYCHOANALYSIS

Psychoanalysis will first be presented in the traditional or classical way, in accordance with what we have called the old model. More contemporary thinking will follow, in accordance with the new model. The trappings of psychoanalysis involve the patient coming for regularly scheduled sessions, four or five times a week, for a number of years. There is no contact between patient and psychoanalyst outside of the appointments. Sessions are conducted with the patient lying on the psychoanalytic couch and the analyst sitting comfortably behind the patient. The patient is instructed simply to free-associate; that is, he is to do his best to say whatever comes to his mind and not eliminate any thoughts for any reason. He is particularly cautioned to try not to eliminate thoughts because he thinks they are silly or irrelevant, because he is fearful that the analyst will disapprove, because he wants to avoid uncomfortable feelings associated with them, or because the thoughts relate to the analyst. Often this is all of the instruction the patient is given.

As the patient tries to free-associate, various resistances within him make the process difficult. As these resistances are noticed by the analyst, she will comment on them in an effort to help the patient overcome them and continue to free-associate. The analyst initially confines her comments to these resistances and to helping the patient to elaborate and expand on what he is saying. Throughout the psychoanalysis the analyst's comments remain of a very specific nature. They are directed specifically to the analytic process and are almost always in the nature of clarifications and interpretations. Almost all comments serve the singular purpose of enhancing the psychoanalytic process. Psychoanalysis works as a very gradual process during which aspects of oneself that were previously unconscious become conscious. The transference is used as the primary and most effective forum for this process. In order to provide a setting in which the patient can most easily transfer his feelings onto the analyst, the analyst has to be seen in a neutral way. It is for this reason that the analyst confines her remarks to clarifications and interpretations regarding the psychoanalytic process as exclusively as possible. The analyst is thus able to maintain her neutral position while still being warm, empathic, and concerned about the patient.

Aided by the frequency and the intensity of the sessions, by the use of the couch and the basic process of free-association, and by the maintenance of a neutral position by the analyst, a progressively intense transference becomes established. This intense transference involves the patient's displacing or transferring onto the analyst feelings and thoughts that were originally directed toward the important people of his early childhood. The transference includes not only these feelings and thoughts, but also defenses against them. It is based on both the actual and fantasized past, as experienced by the patient. The patient's pathological and nonpathological personality traits, as well as his symptoms, all based on intrapsychic conflict, are activated in the psychoanalytic process and become an integral part of the transference. It is the establishment and working through of the transference that is crucial to the attainment of insight, and that most clearly differentiates psychoanalysis from other forms of psychotherapy.

Continuing to confine himself basically to clarifications and interpretations, the analyst begins to comment on aspects of the transference about which the patient is unaware, especially when these appear as resistances to the analytic process. She correlates what is happening in the transference with the patient's current interactions and relationships with significant others, and especially with the patient's significant interactions and relationships in childhood. In this way the analyst helps the patient to begin to learn about previously unconscious aspects of himself, including those aspects that have afforded him the most difficulty. As the patient expands his awareness in this way and gains insight, he is gradually able to make adaptive adjustments and changes in his psychopathology, in his personality, and in his life. The permanency of these changes can be attributed to underlying "structural change," that is, changes in the alignment and relationship of the id, ego, and superego. The analytic process is not smooth; rather, it is characterized by continual resistances and continual progressions and regressions, but with a gradual overall advancement.

Gill (1954), in his classic paper, defined psychoanalysis as a therapeutic technique, employed by a neutral analyst, that permits and results in the development of an intense transference, with the ultimate resolution of this transference by the technique of interpretation alone. There are basically three aspects of this definition that distinguish analysis from other forms of psychotherapy: the analyst's neutrality, the development and resolution of the transference, and the emphasis on interpretation as the primary therapeutic intervention. It is these three aspects that many (Ticho 1970; Kernberg 1980) focus on when differentiating psychoanalysis from other forms of psychotherapy. Given this definition, for analysis to be successful, the patient's personality traits, symptoms, and psychopathology must become activated in the treatment situation, entered into a specific transference with the analyst, and worked through and resolved in the analytic process by interpretation alone. Thus a critical criterion for analyzability is that such a transference can be formed and resolved without disruptive fragmentation or regression. The basically neurotic individual meets this criterion; the basically psychotic individual does not. Kohut (1971, 1984) believes strongly that the narcissistic personality meets this criterion, although some disagree. Whether the borderline individual meets this criterion depends largely on one's criteria for the diagnosis of the borderline patient.

The preceding description of psychoanalysis, traditional and classical as it is, remains a good one for comparing psychoanalysis to other forms of psychotherapy. In contemporary times, however, many take exception to aspects of the traditional view. The positivist position of the classical school, where the analyst is thought capable of standing outside the interaction with the patient in a search for objective truth, has been challenged by newer perspectives. These include relational models, self psychology, intersubjectivity, social constructivism, and postmodern thinking. Many analysts of the classical school have changed some of their views in accordance with these newer ideas.

Thus there is a shift from viewing analysis as a process where the patient transfers his feelings onto a blank screen, to a process more interactional, interpersonal, and subjective in nature, where there is a co-mingling of transference and countertransference between patient and analyst. The analyst, as well as the patient, is viewed as a unique individual with his own theory of how analysis works, his own idiosyncracies, and his own past, all of which contribute to the unfolding of the psychoanalytic process. Some posit the analyst, in addition to the patient, as being involved in the construction of the transference. Many integrate the positivist with more contemporary approaches by conceptualizing the patient as coming to analysis with pre-existing feelings, ideas, and personality traits, which he transfers onto the analyst, who also has pre-existing feelings, ideas, and personality traits that influence and skew the psychoanalytic process.

With these changing perspectives, the concepts of the authority of the analyst and that of neutrality have been questioned. Analysis is sometimes viewed more as a process between coequals than between an uninformed patient and a knowledgeable authority. Some (Hoffman 1996) emphasize a dialectic between the analyst as an authority and the analyst as a person like the patient. Neutrality is now uniformly viewed as an impossible state to attain. Yet, despite this, many hold it as a desirable ideal to try to approximate. Others (Renik 1996) view it as an antiquated and even harmful concept, advocating the acceptance of the nonneutral subjective analyst.

The basic task of analysis, the attainment of insight, or the discovery of that which was previously unconscious, via a reliving in the transference, has also been challenged. The emphasis on empathic attunement and immersion, advocated by some as a means to attain insight, has been posited by others as an end in itself. Some (Renik 1996; Hoffman 1996) believe that learning in analysis takes place dialectically. Dialectics between the authority of the analyst and the analyst as a person similar to the patient, between the analyst's role-defined behavior and his spontaneous expressive participation, between a positivist and intersubjective approach, and between modern and postmodern thinking have been noted as important aspects of the psychoanalytic process. Some feel that the patient learns dialectically by contrasting his thinking with new alternate perspectives proposed by the analyst. A postmodern influence focuses on factors such as uncertainty, ambiguity, ambivalence, fragmentation, irony, cynicism, and relativism. These contemporary ideas might well be confusing to the beginner; they can also be confusing to some sophisticated and experienced therapists.

Psychoanalysis is basically designed for individuals in the normal-neurotic grouping. These individuals include those with symptomatic neuroses, but more frequently are people primarily with character (or personality) pathology. They usually suffer from chronic problems that, although far from disabling, interfere with their attaining their life goals, maximizing their potentials, and leading basically content lives. These individuals suffer from a wide assortment of character problems, including those of obsessive-compulsive, hysterical, depressive, masochistic, narcissistic, and mixed natures.

Although the character pathology varies markedly, these individuals commonly present themselves in one of several ways. One of the most common initial presentations is that of the individual who, although he does well on the job and has many friends, is unable to form sustaining, long-term, intimate personal relationships. Marriage is a goal, but something is stopping him from attaining this goal. This individual realizes that his problems are chronic and deep-seated, and lie within himself. Often he is somewhat sophisticated about psychoanalysis and specifically comes with that treatment modality in mind. This individual frequently, although not always, suffers from sexual difficulties, plus varying degrees of anxiety and depression, in addition to his presenting complaints. A second common initial presentation is that of the patient who, although she performs acceptably at work, feels that something is holding her back and stopping her from living up to her potential. There may be overt problems with her peers or superiors, and there may be anxiety about succeeding. This person also has come to realize that her problems are chronic, deep-seated, and within herself. She may or may not additionally have problems in maintaining long-term, intimate relationships, and may or may not suffer accompanying anxiety or depression.

For individuals who have psychopathology mainly at the neurotic level and who suffer from deep-seated character problems, most obviously manifested in failures in maintaining long-term intimate relationships or in failures in maximizing their potential at work, psychoanalysis is often the treatment of choice. This is also the case for individuals with chronic symptomatic neuroses. For individuals who present clear-cut narcissistic problems, psychoanalysis, although recommended by some, remains controversial. Among individuals in the borderline grouping, psychoanalysis is generally considered only for a selected minority. Psychoanalysis is generally not considered for individuals in the psychotic grouping.

ANALYTICALLY ORIENTED PSYCHOTHERAPY

As elaborated in the previous chapter, the trappings of analytically oriented psychotherapy involve regularly scheduled sessions, usually two but sometimes three a week, held for varying periods of time. As in psychoanalysis, there is basically no contact between patient and psychotherapist outside of the appointments. Sessions are typically conducted with the patient and therapist sitting across from each other in comfortable chairs. The patient is usually told that the sessions are hers; that she can talk about whatever she chooses. In addition to discussing topics of her choice, the patient is encouraged to report seemingly extraneous thoughts and fantasies that occur to her during the sessions. As in psychoanalysis, areas of typical resistance to such discussion are often mentioned. Thus the trappings of analytically oriented psychotherapy are both similar to and different from those of psychoanalysis.

Although the trappings are somewhat different, the therapist attempts to conduct analytically oriented psychotherapy in a manner as similar as possible to that used in psychoanalysis. He tries to remain relatively neutral (in accordance with his concept of neutrality) relies on insight oriented interventions as much as possible, and tries to make maximum therapeutic use of the transference. Just as in psychoanalysis, the therapist comments on resistances, tries to correlate the transference with current interactions and significant childhood relationships, and attempts to help the patient to understand gradually those aspects of herself about which she is unaware. This is analytically oriented psychotherapy in its pure form.

For ideally selected patients, even this pure form of analytically oriented psychotherapy can be limited in effectiveness compared with psychoanalysis. Without the use of the couch, without the process of free-association, and with less frequent sessions, the transference often does not form with the same primitivity, intensity, or speed. Although the ability to form an intense transference varies markedly from patient to patient with individuals in the normal-neurotic grouping, the quality of the transference in analytically oriented psychotherapy is usually not on a par with that in psychoanalysis. Although analytically oriented psychotherapy can be quite effective, it is the lack of a fully developed intense transference that limits this form of psychotherapy. Many individuals undergoing analytically oriented psychotherapy are very similar to those undergoing psychoanalysis. Time and money limitations, fear of psychoanalysis per se, and lack of knowledge about the psychoanalytic process are the usual reasons that psychoanalysis proper is not chosen.

A further word regarding the similarities and differences between analytically oriented psychotherapy and psychoanalysis is in order. Amongst the different schools of psychotherapy, the group that most sharply differentiates psychoanalysis from analytically oriented psychotherapy is the school of ego psychology. Even amongst ego psychologists, however, there are differences of opinion here. One subgroup views these two modalities as uniquely different, whereas another subgroup views the two as separate but on a continuum. The relational school makes the least distinction between the two modalities, viewing them as quite similar. In fact, writers of this school sometimes state that they make no distinctions between psychoanalysis and analytically oriented psychotherapy, at least for the purposes of their articles. Whereas the traditional self psychologists are more similar to the ego psychologists in this regard, many of the contemporary self psychologists are more similar to those of the relational school. The above generalizations are merely impressions, certainly open to dispute.

MODIFIED ANALYTICALLY ORIENTED PSYCHOTHERAPY

Modified analytically oriented psychotherapy involves the same trappings as analytically oriented psychotherapy. Modifications are in the areas that differentiate psychoanalysis from the other forms of psychotherapy: the analyst's neutrality, the development and resolution of the transference, and the emphasis on insight oriented techniques as the primary therapeutic interventions. Modifications are initiated because of the psychopathology of the patient, which makes unmodified analytically oriented psychotherapy difficult-to-impossible. Modified analytically oriented psychotherapy is ideally suited for many borderline individuals.

The area of least modification for borderline patients is the transference, which continues to be emphasized as the crucial forum through which the conflicts of the patient are resolved. This emphasis is especially suitable for these patients, because borderline individuals often form rapid, intense, and sometimes difficult transferences even without the use of the couch. It is the rapid mobilization of the transference that distinguishes the typical borderline patient from the typical neurotic. The latter becomes involved with the transference at a slower and more gradual pace, sometimes with difficulty. The neutrality of the analyst is maintained, not so much regarding equidistance from id, ego, superego, and external reality, but in the sense of the therapist being nonjudgmental, noncritical, and totally focused on the patient. Yet many borderline patients benefit from an interactive and interpersonal style. Modifications regarding interventions vary greatly. In some borderline patients there can be a preponderance of insight oriented interventions; in others the focus switches to supportive techniques.

With the ability of many borderline patients to easily regress and to become rapidly involved with the therapist and the transference, the opportunity to use analytically oriented psychotherapy is clear. However, because of the borderline individual's ego weaknesses and the propensity for too much regression, the modified approach is usually necessary.

DYNAMICALLY ORIENTED PSYCHOTHERAPY

As already elaborated, the trappings of dynamically oriented psychotherapy involve regularly scheduled sessions, often one but sometimes two a week, held for varying periods of time. There is little contact between patient and psychotherapist outside of the appointments. Sessions are always conducted with the patient and therapist sitting across from each other. Basically the same instructions are given to the patient as in analytically oriented psychotherapy, although sometimes the instruction to report seemingly extraneous material is omitted.

The main difference between dynamically oriented psychotherapy and analytically oriented psychotherapy is the down-playing of the transference as a therapeutic modality in the former. Although transference reactions are noted, especially when they occur as resistances, the elaboration of the transference is not considered a major ingredient in this form of psychotherapy. Rather, the therapist and the patient focus much more exclusively on present-day interactions and relationships, and their correlation to the patient's past. Patient and therapist together try to understand the patient's present-day interactions on the basis of her sensitivities, vulnerabilities, and distortions, which originate in the past. A positive therapeutic alliance is fostered, and the therapist is sometimes mildly idealized. Occasional suggestion and education are employed, along with the insight oriented interventions.

Dynamically oriented psychotherapy is found particularly useful by some psychotherapists for a selected group of patients, often psychotic, but sometimes borderline, who present problems with the elaboration and working through of the transference. There is one group of borderline patients who start psychotherapy with a modified analytically oriented approach, then after a reasonable therapeutic alliance has been established, switch to a dynamically oriented modality. Other psychotherapists routinely use dynamically oriented psychotherapy as their primary form of psychotherapy, both for patients who would benefit from a more analytically oriented approach and for those who would not.

As previously noted, there is debate about what type of psychotherapy is best for neurotic patients who are not in psychoanalysis. One group favors simulating analysis as much as possible. A second group, noting the difficulty in attaining transference regressions with neurotic patients in psychotherapy, favors using a dynamically oriented approach. Other therapists lean toward an analytically oriented modality for those neurotic patients (often hysterical in personality type) who can form an intense transference in psychotherapy, while employing a more dynamically oriented model for those neurotic patients (often obsessive in personality type) who have greater difficulty here.

SUPPORTIVE PSYCHOTHERAPY

In supportive psychotherapy the patient comes for regularly scheduled sessions—usually once a week but sometimes more frequently—for varying, but often, lengthy periods. The principle underlying the number of sessions scheduled is virtually the opposite of that used in the more analytically oriented psychotherapies. In the latter approaches, increased sessions are used to promote intensity. In supportive psychotherapy the goal is to inhibit intensity, especially when it leads to unwanted symptoms and problematic behavior. Here more frequent sessions are employed to stem untoward regression, at times when the patient is having acute difficulty with some of his basic ego functions. When the patient is doing well, a lower frequency of sessions, usually once a week, generally suffices. In supportive psychotherapy, contact between patient and therapist outside the sessions is promoted only to the extent that it is necessary. Sessions are always conducted with the patient and therapist sitting across from each other. Instructions to the patient are simply to discuss those events in his life with which he is having difficulty.

Supportive psychotherapy is best suited for individuals with active disturbances in a number of their ego functions. This form of psychotherapy is indicated for a large group of basically psychotic individuals, although another large group of psychotic patients can benefit more from dynamically oriented psychotherapy, at least some of the time. Supportive psychotherapy is also used by some in the treatment of selected borderline individuals. This form of psychotherapy is sometimes supplemented by psychiatric medication.

The purpose of supportive psychotherapy is to help build up the patient's weak ego functions, hence the often-used term ego building. For this purpose many types of therapeutic intervention are employed, including education, suggestion, clarification, reassurance, advice, and instruction, but not usually interpretation. For these interventions to be most successful, the maintenance of a positive transference and a therapeutic alliance is exceptionally important. For this reason, the transference is usually not discussed unless it is a resistance. Likewise, transference distortions are often rapidly corrected by education and reality testing. For this kind of psychotherapy to proceed optimally, free-association is not wanted. What is wanted is a detailed description of the day-to-day events that led to the patient's current difficulty with his ego functions. Hence, contrary to the more analytically oriented approaches, the focus is on the here and now, and reporting of weekly events is encouraged.

The initial goal of supportive psychotherapy is to help the patient strengthen and maintain his ego functioning so that he can adapt adequately in day-to-day interactions. When the patient begins to function acceptably in this realm, further goals are added. A second and more difficult goal is to help the patient identify and accept those areas in which he is sensitive and vulnerable to regression. Once these areas are identified and accepted by the patient, he can begin to deal with them more effectively. The tasks of helping the patient to identify these stressful areas and then to deal more effectively with them can be very time consuming. As this work is pursued, the psychotherapeutic approach often becomes more exploratory and switches to a dynamically oriented framework. If and when the patient is able to make this switch, it is considered a welcome psychotherapeutic advance.

Chapter Eight

Projective Identification, Enactment, and the Transference

The concepts of projective identification and enactment are commonly invoked but often misunderstood. In relation to the transference, some therapists, especially those with traditional backgrounds, do not invoke either of these concepts. Others, however, view either projective identification or enactments as essential aspects of the transference. A number of therapists, particularly those of the Kleinian persuasion, view psychotherapy as a series of interactions between patient and therapist, all based on projective identifications. The patient projects onto the therapist, interacts with the therapist in accordance with the projection, then reintrojects an altered version of the projection. The reintrojected version differs from the original in that it has been processed and modified by the therapist. The patient then makes another projection onto the therapist, and the same process occurs. This process repeats itself throughout the psychotherapy. Thus psychotherapy is conceptualized as an unending series of projections and reintrojections, with change taking place via this process. Change in this regard is related to the extent to which the projections are modified before reintrojection.

Other therapists (Katz 1998; Renik 1993) view psychotherapy as an unending series of transference/countertransference enactments. The thinking here is that on some level, often subtle and unconscious, the patient is always responding in accordance with the way the therapist acts. Correspondingly, the therapist is always responding to the way the patient acts. All these responses, whether subtle or overt, are regarded as enactments. Thus, transference/countertransference enactments are continual and play a decisive role in the psychotherapy process.

PROJECTIVE IDENTIFICATION

Because the concepts of enactment and particularly projective identification can be elusive, especially to the beginner, this chapter will focus on clarifying these terms, beginning with projective identification. Melanie Klein (1946) first described projective identification as a process beginning in the earliest time of life, in a phase she called the paranoid-schizoid position. Klein was referring to a process in which parts of the self are split off and projected into another person, leading to a particular kind of identification. This process includes an effort to control the other person by the projected parts. Segal (1964) summarized Klein's original description of projective identification succinctly: "Parts of the self and internal objects are split off and projected into the external object, which then becomes possessed by, controlled and identified with the projected parts" (p. 27). The concept of projective identification has been developed and elaborated by many of Klein's followers, including Bion (1959a, 1959b), Rosenfeld (1952, 1954), and Segal (1964). Later contributions along these lines have been made by Malin and Grotstein (1966), Grotstein (1981), Ogden (1979, 1982, 1986), and others.

Although always an important concept in the Kleinian school of psychoanalysis, the term projective identification attained increasing popularity and became more generally widespread with the publication of Kernberg's work on the borderline personality organization (1967). Kernberg listed projective identification as one of the borderline defenses, together with splitting, primitive idealization, primitive denial, omnipotence and devaluation.

A common way of thinking about projective identification is as follows (Goldstein 1991): a projection is followed by an interpersonal interaction in which the projector actively pressures the recipient to think, feel, and act in accordance with the projection. It is the coercive interpersonal interaction that is the essential feature of projective identification. Confusion occurs because different therapists view the process of projective identification in different ways. To look at the different current usages, a broad model of projective identification will be utilized as a point of reference. This broad model is in accordance with the work of Ogden (1979, 1982), who originally defined projective identification as a process occurring in three steps. Step 1 involves the fantasy of projecting a part of oneself into another person, with that part controlling the person from within. The projected part is something the individual wishes to be rid of, either because the part threatens to destroy the self from within or because the person feels the part is in danger of attack by other aspects of the self. A distinction is made here between projective identification and projection. In projective identification, the projector feels at one with the recipient of the projection; this feeling of oneness involves a blurring of self and object representations. In contrast, in projection proper, the projector feels estranged from and threatened by the recipient of the projection.

Step 2 is an interpersonal interaction in which the projector actively pressures the recipient to think, feel, and act in accordance with the projection. According to Ogden, projective identification does not exist when there is no interaction of this nature.

Finally, in Step 3, the projection is reinternalized after it has been psychologically processed by the recipient. The nature of the reinternalization process depends on the maturational level of the projector and can range from primitive types of introjection to mature forms of identification. Whatever the process, the reinternalization offers the projector the potential for attaining new ways of handling a set of feelings and fantasies that he or she could only wish to be rid of in the past.

Later, Ogden (1986) clarified that the projection can involve either a self representation or an object representation. He deemphasized the concept of controlling the person from within and backed away from the need for a blurring of self and object representations as necessary to the process. With these recent clarifications, Ogden's concept of projective identification provides a current broad model of projection.

Some (Kernberg 1987a, 1987b; Sandler 1987) feel that Ogden's concept of projective identification is too broad. However, it is just that aspect of his work which makes it conducive as a reference to compare the various current usages of projective identification. In using his work as a reference, we will modify and outline Ogden's steps in the following fashion: Step 1 is the projection (or externalization) of part of oneself onto an external object (recipient). Step 1a is the blurring of self and object representations. Step 2 is the interpersonal interaction in which the projector actively pressures the recipient to think, feel, and act in accordance with the projection. Step 3 is the reinternalization of the projection after the projection has been psychologically processed (and modified) by the recipient.

As will be shown, the different definitions of projective identification relate to exactly how one conceptualizes the term projection in Step 1, whether Step 1a is deemed necessary, and how many of the three steps are required for the process to qualify as projective identification.

Step 1: The Projection

What is meant by the term projection is very important because people who use the term projective identification differ in their definition of projection. Sandler (1987) defines projection as involving a transfer of mental content from a self representation to an object representation. Meissner (1980) is basically in agreement with this, stating that projection involves an attribution of part of a self representation to an object representation. Meissner further distinguishes displacement from projection, stating that displacement involves an attribution of part of one object representation to another object representation. Differentiation of projection from displacement in this way is sometimes the norm. Yet Ogden (1979, 1982), in accordance with many in the Kleinian school, classifies displacement (of one object representation to another) as a form of projection. The question of the definition of projection is crucial here, because the process of projective identification takes on different meanings in accordance with whether the projection is a self or object representation. In general, the projection of a self representation is thought to constitute a more primitive process than the projection of an object representation. Projections of self representations, when they occur frequently, are most typical of individuals with borderline and psychotic disorders. Regarding the psychotherapeutic process, these types of projections may occur in neurotic individuals, especially in intense transferences; however, with the neurotic individual they are neither frequent nor predominant. In contrast, in psychotherapy with patients with borderline and psychotic disorders, these kinds of projections can be frequent.

The projection of object representations constitutes a different phenomenon. Traditionally, when one thinks of the transference as a repetition of actual relations from the past, fantasized relations from the past, and defense against both, one is referring to projections of object representations. Projections of object representations are ubiquitous; they are commonplace among all individuals, both in day-to-day interactions and within psychotherapy. As noted, projections of object representations are synonymous with displacements.

If only projections of self representations are included in the definition of projective identification, it refers mostly to a process involving individuals with borderline and psychotic disorders. This process, often thought to include some blurring of ego boundaries, is basically in accordance with Kernberg's original thinking (1987a, 1987b) and that of Meissner (1980). If projections of object representations are included in the definition of projective identification, and if blurring of ego boundaries is not required, then projective identification refers to a process in which perhaps all individuals engage. This is in accordance with the work of Grotstein (1981) and with Ogden's more recent use of the term (1986). Both Ogden and Grotstein basically view projective identification as a universal feature of the transference.

Step 1a: The Blurring of Self and Object Representations

It is interesting that both Kernberg (1967, 1975) and Ogden (1979, 1982) originally emphasized the blurring of self and object representations as part of projective identification, then moved away from including it in the definition. In more recent descriptions of projective identification by Kernberg (1987a, 1987b) and Ogden (1986), the blurring of self and object representations has been conspicuously omitted, although neither author states the reasons for the omission.

In his original concept of projective identification, Kernberg (1967) stated that it was the lack of ego boundaries per se that led to the identification that followed the projection. The beauty of Kernberg's original concept, in applying it to patients with borderline disorders, is that these patients often exhibit blurring of ego boundaries in close interpersonal relationships, enabling projections in that context to take on the characteristics of projective identification. As stated, in later writings Kernberg (1987a, 1987b) has removed Step 1a from his definition of projective identification. Although in his view projective identification is a more primitive defense than projection itself, it is no longer considered an exclusively psychotic mechanism. However, in Kernberg's view, projective identification continues to be typical of individuals with borderline and psychotic disorders and not typical of neurotic individuals.

Like Kernberg, Ogden originally emphasized that in projective identification, "the person involved in such a process is operating at least in part at a developmental level wherein there is profound blurring of boundaries between self and object representations" (1979, p. 352). Later, however, Ogden (1986) omits this blurring of ego boundaries when he describes projective identification. Certainly, in viewing projective identification as a universal feature of the transference, Ogden no longer thinks in terms of blurring of self and object representations.

In accordance with the discussion of Step 1, the blurring of ego boundaries in projective identification might be related to the nature of the projection. Projections of object representations basically do not include the blurring of ego boundaries. However, projections of self representations do include such a blurring. When one thinks about it, the transfer of a self representation to an object representation implies blurring of self and object representations by definition.

Step 2: The Interpersonal Interaction

In this step, pressure is exerted by the projector on the recipient of the projection to think, feel, and act in accordance with the projection. Although some limit their concept of projective identification to Steps 1 and 1a only, most feel that Step 2 is crucial in the projective identification process. Ogden states that "projective identification does not exist where there is no interaction between projector and object" (1979, p. 359). Step 2 actually expands the concept of projective identification beyond the intrapsychic into the realm of interpersonal. In that regard, Ogden (1979, 1982) views projective identification as a bridging concept, one that links phenomena in the intrapsychic sphere with those in the interpersonal.

As noted, not everyone is happy with this expansion. In this regard, Meissner (1980) differentiates between the one-body context (intrapsychic) and two-or-more body context (interpersonal). Meissner regards projective identification as a totally intrapsychic phenomenon and limits his concept to Steps 1 and 1a. Kernberg (1987) minimizes Meissner's differentiation, stating that it is artificial to separate the intrapsychic from the interpersonal. Despite this, Kernberg's original definition of projective identification (1967) is basically an intrapsychic one, whereas his more recent definition (1987a, 1987b) clearly includes an interpersonal component.

Sandler (1987) helps us understand the various usages of projective identification by classifying projective identification into three stages, in accordance with the historical usages of the term. In Stage 1, in accordance with Meissner, the processes remain intrapsychic. In Stage 2, the therapist becomes involved in the interaction (Step 2) by identifying with the projection to a degree sufficient to contribute to the analyst's countertransference. Here, the therapist is influenced by the projection only by his or her identification; the patient does not actively pressure the analyst to receive the projection. It is only in Stage 3 that there is a definite interaction, where the therapist is pressured to act in accordance with the projection. In this stage, the opportunity for reinternalization becomes available.

Step 3: The Reinternalization of the Projection

In Step 3, the projection is reinternalized after it has been psychologically processed and altered by the recipient. The psychological processing is in accordance with the recipient's psychic structure. If the recipient is sufficiently different from the projector, the processed version of the original projection might include substantial change. According to Ogden (1979, 1982), the processed version might be modified in such a way that the projector, after the reinternalization, might no longer feel the need to be rid of the now altered projection. Regarding psychotherapy, although the processing of the projection is often thought to take place silently, interpretations regarding the projection can also be used to influence the reinternalization. The exact nature of the reinternalization process depends on the maturational level of the projector, and can vary from primitive types of introjection to more mature forms of identification.

Step 3 extends the concept of projective identification even further. This step has particular relevance to the psychotherapeutic process. The reinternalization process offers the projector the potential for change, for attaining new ways of handling a set of feelings and fantasies that he or she could only wish to be rid of in the past. With that in mind, some (Grotstein 1981) have understood the essence of psychotherapeutic change as taking place through a series of projective identifications. The developmental process can be conceptualized in an analogous way.

As might be expected, the expansion of projective identification to Step 3 is certainly not uniformly agreed upon. As noted, Meissner (1980) confines his definition of projective identification solely to an intrapsychic process, including Steps 1 and 1a only. Kernberg (1987a, 1987b), although he includes Step 2 in his definition of projective identification, feels that Step 3 would extend the definition too far. Sandler (1987) includes the reinternalization process only in what he calls Stage 3 of projective identification. Despite these differences, the reinternalization process is now commonly included by many in thinking about projective identification.

Regarding the reinternalization process in psychotherapy, change usually can be noted only after the accumulation of a number of instances of reinternalization of projections. This is illustrated in the following case vignette. Ms. D, although she functioned in a highly competitive fashion and was widely respected in her profession, frequently presented herself in psychotherapy as inadequate, ineffective, little, and pathetic. She said she was a loser, was inferior to her colleagues, and was looked down upon and scorned by her fellow professionals. Ms. D insisted that her therapist view her in the same way that she saw herself and repetitively acted to get him to feel and to treat her that way. In a manner particularly annoying to the therapist, Ms. D acted as if it were a fact that the therapist agreed that she was little and inadequate. She elaborated one example after another, based on the assumption that the therapist agreed with her. If the therapist made any comment indicating that he felt differently, Ms. D would argue with him and insist that he was being stupid and demeaning. The therapist felt pressured, coerced, overwhelmed, frustrated, and angry.

Here Ms. D retains her self representation as a little, pathetic, devalued professional while projecting onto the therapist an object representation of a demeaning, devaluing, and critical parent. Note that the self representation is retained; it is the object representation (of someone who treats Ms. D in accordance with her self representation) that is projected. Ms. D here interacts very provocatively with the therapist as she tries to get him to accept her projection.

Regarding the reinternalization process, as Ms. D repetitively insists that the therapist view her as little and inadequate, the therapist is partially influenced by what Ms. D says (that is, by her projections onto him); yet his basic view of her as competent and high powered remains. With time, Ms. D is able to somewhat alter her self representation because of the reinternalization process. To be more specific, Ms. D repetitively projects onto the therapist an object representation of someone who views her in accordance with her self representation. The therapist is able to receive Ms. D's projections but is minimally influenced by them; he maintains his basic view of her as competent and high powered. One could say that he modifies the projections onto him in accordance with his original view. By accumulative reinternalizations of the modified projections, Ms. D is gradually able to alter her self representation in accordance with the way the therapist views her. Thus, she is gradually able to see herself as less little and pathetic and more competent and high powered.

The reinternalization process provides the silent change that can take place by projective identifications. In addition to the silent change, the therapist can make active interventions demonstrating the process of projective identification. Often it is the interpersonal interaction component that is most conducive to initial intervention. In the case of Ms. D, the therapist could intervene in the following way.

> *Therapist:* I want to take a moment and point out what I think might be happening here. I have the feeling you might disagree with me, but I ask you to listen to what I say, then to view my ideas as one possibility. You have been presenting yourself as inferior and inadequate, a loser, as you call it. You have presented a number of reasons why you think this is so. Regarding this, there are two phenomena I want you to consider. The first is that you seem to be doing everything possible to get me to believe that negative view of yourself. You are arguing with me vigorously, and you seem to be trying to force me to feel that way. Second, you then act as if I have accepted that view of you, although I haven't said anything indicating that.

PROJECTIVE IDENTIFICATION VERSUS PROJECTION

A few additional words might be useful to further clarify the confusing distinction between projective identification and projection. As already discussed, some (Kernberg 1987a, 1987b) view projective identification as a more primitive process than projection, one that implies at least some blurring of ego boundaries in the area of the projection. It is this blurring of ego boundaries that causes the projector to hold onto, feel at one with, and continue to identify with the projection. In contrast, projection is seen as occurring when there are clearly differentiated ego boundaries. Here the projector feels little identification with the projection and may distance himself or herself and stay away from the object of the projection.

Others (Hamilton 1988; Ramchandani 1991) are not in agreement here. They note that in projection proper there is a clear loss of reality testing, as demonstrated by a conviction that an aspect of the self is in another person. In projective identification, by contrast, the loss of reality testing is not total, as some lack of clarity remains about the location of the self representation. Additionally, projection proper is most characteristic of severely disturbed psychotic patients, whereas projective identification is more characteristic of less disturbed borderline patients. With these differences in mind, projection proper is viewed as a more primitive mechanism than projective identification. The logic behind Hamilton's and Ramchandani's argument is clear.

Possibly one might speak of three levels of projection, from most primitive to most advanced: psychotic projection, projective identification, and neurotic projection. Psychotic projection would correspond to the type of projection described by Hamilton and Ramchandani; neurotic projection would correspond to the type of projection described by Kernberg.

With the broadening of the definition of projective identification (with the inclusion of object representations as well as self representations in Step 1, and with the elimination of Step 1a as a requirement), the distinction between projective identification and projection is less clear. The extreme here is the elimination of the distinction, as in the idea of Malin and Grotstein (1966), that the projector always retains some contact (and identification) with what is projected. In essence, the distinction between projective identification and projection varies in accordance with the definition of projective identification.

ENACTMENTS

The concept of enactment has become quite popular in psychotherapy of late. Although less confusing than projective identification, some clarification is in order. Enactments are "symbolic interactions between therapists and patients which have unconscious meaning to both" (Chused 1991). Usually an action by the patient is followed by a response from the therapist. Both action and response are primarily unconsciously determined. Although usually initiated by the patient, enactments can also be triggered by the therapist. Once considered the result of unwanted countertransference reactions, enactments today are generally considered inevitable and ubiquitous, constituting an integral part of psychotherapy.

When undetected, enactments can be problematic. When noted, explored, and understood, they clearly contribute to the psychotherapy process. The role of the therapist is to understand his own contribution (as much as possible), then to help the patient to determine her role. It is the understanding afforded by the enactment, and not the enactment itself, that enhances the psychotherapy process. Some enactments, however, provide a shared experience and an increased sense of collaboration that are themselves helpful. Additionally the patient's sense of efficacy in being able to influence the therapist can play a constructive role.

The distinction between enactment and projective identification is sometimes made. Basically, the concepts are similar with minor differences. The concept of projective identification does not demand a response by the therapist, whereas the concept of enactment does. This difference, of course, disappears if the therapist responds. Additionally, the term projective identification places more emphasis on the "coercive" interpersonal interaction. Enactments, by contrast, are often more subtle in nature. Whereas some see psychotherapy as an unending series of projective identifications, others view psychotherapy as an unending series of enactments.

We conclude this chapter with some further thoughts, selective and limited, related to the concept of enactment. The term enactment unites the concepts of transference and acting out. It de-emphasizes obvious exaggerated behaviors, giving greater focus to more subtle actualizations that inevitably occur between patient and therapist (Katz 1998). Involving as participants both partners in the therapeutic dyad, an enactment can express rich combinations of meaning derived from the unconscious minds of both parties.

The tendency of certain patients to act out is a well known phenomenon. The acting-out patient is often one who suffered loss or trauma at an early age, before he was capable of representing his experiences verbally. Such early experiences, never consciously registered as verbal symbols, can later be expressed in action language. Yet, not only patients who have been traumatized at a preverbal age act out. Almost everyone in therapy transitions at times from a narrative verbal modality toward actual dramatization (Loewald 1975). Rather than merely talking about oneself symbolically, patients demonstrate meaning in behavior and action. When a patient behaves in this way, the therapist frequently responds in a similar manner.

Some (Katz 1998; Renik 1993) believe that at least intermittent movement of the psychotherapeutic couple into such enactments is inevitable. Recall Sandler's (1976) concept of role responsiveness, by which the therapist unconsciously responds to the patient's attempts to recreate an infantile role-relationship. Sandler showed how the therapist may unintentionally contribute to the realization of a jointly created enactment that may be largely unconscious to both parties. Extending this idea, we can assume that each member of the therapeutic pair, unconsciously seeking to provoke some interaction, reciprocally impacts and affects the other. The effect of each upon the other is evocative and specific as determined by each party's unique unconscious.

Mitchell (1988) describes how the therapist is "embedded within the [patient's] relational matrix. There is no way for the therapist to avoid his assigned roles and configurations. . . . He plays assigned roles even if he desperately tries to stand outside the patient's system and play no role at all" (p. 292). Perhaps, as Renik (1993) states, psychotherapy inevitably involves a series of enactments which cannot be avoided, occurring in relation to the needs of both partners. Katz (1998) offers a useful idea here. Instead of seeing acting out or enactment as discrete episodes, he proposes the conceptualization of a continuous enacted dimension of the psychotherapeutic process, running alongside of and dialectically interweaving with a verbally symbolized dimension.

Part III

CLINICAL VIGNETTES

Chapter Nine

Love for the Therapist: Analytically Oriented Psychotherapy

INTRODUCTION

Transference can be conceptualized broadly as a universal phenomenon, ubiquitous throughout every person's life, appearing in all relationships. The patient's relationship to the therapist is not anything intrinsically unique in its nature, being distinguished only by the manner in which it is handled (Brenner 1982). Rather than responding in the usual social fashion, the therapist proposes that transference thoughts and feelings be examined for the sake of understanding. As early as 1915, Freud held that transference love essentially is of the same nature as love experienced elsewhere. What distinguishes love in the therapeutic setting is that, as far as the patient knows, it is not reciprocated, but goes unrequited. According to Kernberg (1995), while neurotic love that is unrequited increases in attachment, in transference love the attachment is resolved through mourning.

In classical theory, a person seeking love in part is unconsciously searching to "re-find" earlier love objects, whether the mother of earliest infancy, or the romantically idealized but forbidden parent of later childhood, or both. Childhood conflicts over strivings for exclusive possession of the parent inevitably play out again in later love relations. Transference love for the therapist quite often emerges as a natural development within the conducive treatment setting, and may intensify to a full-blown "transference neurosis", where the childhood conflicts are reactivated and engaged intensively in the relationship with the therapist. While the positive experience and expression of love for the therapist may thus be a natural development, a patient's insistence on erotic fulfilment with the therapist may also defend against awareness of opposite tendencies directed toward him, such as angry and destructive urges, feelings and fantasies. Persisting deep love for the therapist also may serve as resistance against accepting frustration of the "transferred" infantile wishes, which may have never been fully renounced. The patient eventually must relinquish claims to what is impossible to achieve. The playing out and working through of such conflicts in the transference may involve countless interactions involving hope, wish, frustration, disappointment, anger, contrition, reflection, remembering, and grieving. It is through resolution of old losses and traumata, and through arriving at new solutions to old conflicts, that the patient gains liberation from old ties and old solutions, and gains freedom to advance on to other, new life goals and relationships.

From the more recent perspective, which emphasizes that the patient-therapist relationship is also something new and real in itself, intense love and desire in the transference may offer an avenue to deeper self-actualization. This profound experience may help build intrapsychic tolerance and capacity for intense affects, not only of lust but also of longing, tenderness and concern, feelings which the patient previously may have needed to deny. In the context of the transference relationship, someone may, for the first time, experience and explore a sense of interpersonal closeness, vitality, and also responsibility. Love can expand the reaches of interpersonal imagination.

Hopefully, the therapist can tolerate internally the natural development of his own erotic fantasies, should they occur in response to the patient's love, without needing either to deny or undo them (e.g., by rejecting the patient), or to act on them. The patient's urges to enact the vividly alive intrapsychic scenario, however, may prompt the therapist to defend against awareness of aspects of himself activated by the patient's "projective identifications". He may experience powerful pressure or temptation to depart from his professional stance and join the patient in treating the love as "real". Maintaining the professional frame and limitations of the treatment provides the protection for the two of them necessary to ensure against acting out, while also permitting maximal freedom to explore the full range of feelings, fantasies and identifications activated.

The therapist's role is multifold. He must at the same time see the situation from both the intrapsychic and the interpersonal perspectives. He aims to address the patient's defenses against the full development of the transference, while neither phobically avoiding, nor seductively or intrusively stimulating the patient's feelings. Patient and therapist eventually will need to explore both the patient's love and also his or her reactions to the frustrations of its being unreciprocated and unconsummated (Kernberg 1995). The therapist aims to maintain in himself and to model for the patient that "dual state of awareness" (Gabbard 1994) by which he both permits experience of the intensity and urgency of the feelings as real, but also remains cognitively aware of the need to understand rather than to act out.

Ultimately, the old and new conceptualizations of transference differ primarily in emphasis. Despite the differences, both views acknowledge that transference love is both something new, and also a revival of the meaningful fantasies and memories of relationships from the past. Understanding how these dimensions of past and present recontextualize one another is an important part of the therapeutic work. Yet, insofar as the old and new views suggest differing approaches to how one actually should intervene with a patient, the ambiguity in distinguishing past from present in the transference may create uncertainty about what technical approach is the best to pursue, a dilemma confronted in the case presented here.

CASE PRESENTATION

A 28-year-old single woman, a government administrator, had been in therapy with a male therapist for a number of years at once per week. For all intents and purposes, the patient presented herself as meek, homely, nonambitious, extremely timid, and shy, especially around men. Quite striking early on was her inability to look at the therapist directly: she'd glance at him, and then avert her eyes; this was explored extensively for its various meanings. She'd had a number of relationships, but never any one that was very promising for marriage. She recurrently had felt let down by men. In one significant affair several years ago, she became involved with an older, wealthy married man, but realized over time that he was simply "using" her. When she began to make greater demands, he "dropped me like a hot potato." She, however, had great trouble letting go.

Her father had been a powerful business executive, often traveling to Europe. She idolized him, but remembered sadness, depression, and longing for her father during the months that he was overseas. Her mother, depressed and irritable, would stay home with her and her younger brother. When she was twelve, however, her father took her along for a summer to Paris, London, and Bonn, just the two of them. She was thrilled to be his companion at elegant hotels and to be introduced by him to his powerful friends and colleagues. Yet, it was at this time that she began to realize that her father had other female companionship, and it was during this trip that she stumbled upon his pornographic magazines. Her parents divorced when she was fourteen, and her father quickly remarried a younger woman, who the patient felt resented her. She later became quite angry and resentful when she would visit her father and stepmother, and found him prevented from giving her as much attention and generosity as she believed he wanted to, presumably because of the stepmother's interference.

For the first year and a half of treatment, much work focused on the patient's avoidance of relationships with men in general, and also her resistance to awareness of transference feelings. Eventually, at about two years of therapy, she said, "I know you feel that I should get into a relationship with a man and eventually get married, and I worry that I will disappoint you, and you'll feel let down by me if I don't do that. But I'm not sure that I want to. I don't trust men. They're only interested in women for sex. And I feel that men have such an advantage over me, because I need them so much, and they don't need me at all. They can have sex without love, but for me, to have sex with somebody necessarily makes me love them. So I'm not interested in that agenda. I think I'm better off just being alone. I can entertain myself very well. I come here because I love you. Sometimes, I think that you love me too, and it makes me angry that you still hold to your professional detachment. I know that you would hate yourself if you gave in and had a relationship with me, so I know that it's impossible, but that only makes it more frustrating. But I think about you all the time, and that's not helping me move forward with my life goals."

The therapist asked if perhaps being so extremely preoccupied with him was defending against permitting herself to get involved in a real relationship outside of the therapy. She chuckled and said, "Yes, but what's going to defend me against the defense?" She felt increasingly frustrated at her feelings of love for the therapist, which she felt he would not reciprocate, and she said, "What's the point of coming to therapy only to feel frustrated? My attraction toward you is too strong."

The therapist, within himself wary of temptation, felt professionally obligated to be "proper," and this may have created in his manner at such times a certain stilted quality. He said, "You're realizing that nothing can happen between us besides doing therapy. Of course, it's difficult to feel so frustrated and disappointed, but maybe those feelings are interfering with moving on." The patient made no objection to this comment, but went on talking about the futility of her love for the therapist. Several days later, however, she broke off the treatment precipitously, informing the therapist with merely a curtly apologetic note. The therapist felt rejected, sad, and angry with himself, thinking that he had erred somehow, perhaps in not appreciating more directly the genuineness and depth of her wishes for him. Pressing that they should "move on" (e.g., to memories of her father, or to her concerns about potential relationships with other men) may have seemed to express his fear and denial of her feeling. He felt that he might have pushed her away because he felt unable to tolerate and explore further with her the reality of the transference in the here-and-now. She had rejected him for rejecting her.

Notice how her feelings toward the therapist, who, to her, was an obviously older, "powerful, more wealthy man", repeated a pattern seen first in her worshipful relationship for her father, then for the married paramour. This could have been interpreted to her correctly, but, on the other hand, the therapist had feared that such an interpretation might also have constituted "fleeing to the past", to escape the intensity and immediacy of the real feelings and wishes she was expressing.

The therapist, moreover, was now reflecting on how his countertransference fears and defensiveness had interfered with his optimal therapeutic functioning, facilitating the patient's flight from treatment instead of her deeper exploration. He recalled how his mother seductively had treated him as her "special child", both enthralling but also controlling him. By adolescence, he had reacted with obstinacy, rejecting and depreciating her. He wondered if in the countertransference, he had experienced and treated the patient, who emphasized how "special" he was to her, as if she were the "threatening mother."

Some four months later, he was surprised and pleased when the patient called to ask if she could come back "for one session." In that session she said, "I knew that I would miss you, but didn't think it would be as painful as it was. It was depressing to me not to be able to see you. So, I'm wondering what to do. I can see that I need to have somebody in my life, but I think that men are jerks, and I don't think that I can trust them. I don't believe that marriage is intrinsically likely to hold together. Half end in divorce, and the others probably are barely kept together. And it seems that I would be at such a disadvantage if I depended on a man, but I can't tolerate the idea of a man depending on me. I wish I were gay! But my curse is that I am not." In various statements (not all at once) the therapist said that he wondered if she feared that if she returned to therapy, she might become too dependent on him; maybe that was part of her reason for having broken off the treatment in the first place. She perhaps felt that he had been "using" her, letting her reveal her feelings for him, while he gave her back nothing of the sort. Maybe she was angry that he was frustrating her, not responding to her openness in kind. Even worse, though, would be any possibility that he would come to depend on her. She felt that she needed to keep away to avoid these frustrations and fears, but that would leave her with so many feelings and issues unresolved; clearly, these were affecting her possibilities for happiness.

Thus, in the manner of analytically oriented therapy, the therapist interpreted within the transference. He was making it clear that her action, breaking off the therapy, was understandable as a response to transference feelings and fantasies that she wished to avoid. She had resisted further deepening the exploration which ultimately could provide the growth she needed. Notice that he did not mention at all his subsequent understanding of how his counter-transference had contributed to his stilted reactions. To refer to his own past problems with his mother, he knew, would have been to burden the patient with his own "issues," significantly distracting her from her efforts at self-understanding. Still, he thought he might have referred to her perceptions of his awkwardness. For example, he could have said, "Perhaps you imagined that I was frightened of your feelings and wishes for me."

The patient decided to return, "for a while." Over several months, they further explored her conflicts regarding men. In one session, she said, "I just don't really think that I am ever going to want to be married. It's just not worth it. I'm happy enough by myself. But then, what am I coming here for? I think to entertain myself. I love you and sometimes I think that you love me. It feels very good to be here. It's kind of odd." Then there was a pause. After a while, she said, "It's kind of like pornography."

The therapist asked, "How do you mean?"

"I come here to entertain myself, and it's very stimulating. Of course, it's also very frustrating. I think I've told you that when I come here I get aroused, and it's difficult to go home and not have somebody to help me with that."

There was another long pause, after which the therapist asked, "Is this difficult for you to talk about?"

The patient went on, "Yes, it is. Sometimes I think that you want me the way that I want you, but you won't let yourself express that. Part of the reason that I came back to therapy was that I thought to myself, "You've said everything to him, and still he didn't come around to joining you. But you haven't thrown yourself at him physically yet." At this she burst into laughter. "I wonder if I did do that, if I could finally win you over, but it frightens me to think of being rejected; you could tell me to sit down again, or push me away, and then I would feel really bad."

The therapist was conscious, as he had been on previous occasions with her such as this, of feeling attracted to the patient, and recognized guiltily that she was succeeding in being stimulating for him. She was correctly inferring his feelings for her and inviting him to share them with her, but this he knew would be a terrible transgression of necessary therapeutic boundaries. He moreover did not want merely to indulge in enjoying the feelings between them, even silently to himself, for he worried that to do so would be, in effect, "joining in the pornography". On the other hand, he faced a dilemma: How not to seem to be rejecting of her thoughts and feelings as they were actually emerging, without, on the other hand, encouraging her in some mutual seductiveness? He said, "Of course, you think there are limits to what we can do here, but do you feel, though, that there are limits to what you can express in words?"

The patient laughed and said, "I realize that there are not supposed to be, but I find it difficult. It's very frustrating to be feeling this way and not to be able to do anything about it, and I wish that you would help me. I know that you can't. But the fact that sometimes I believe that you really want to, that you love me and are attracted to me, is even more frustrating. So I wonder, what's the point of my coming? This is just entertaining myself, but ultimately, it's very frustrating."

The therapist now realized that she was being subtly coercive with him; she was expressing and inducing pleasurable erotic feelings, chiding him for withholding himself from her, subtly threatening another departure. While feeling affection her, he also began to feel a little angry. Hers was a siren song that he feared would draw him to his own destruction, if he yielded to her appeal. Thinking it was fair to use her own expression, he said, "I wonder what thoughts you have about making the therapy, in effect, into a pornography show? It's as if you are on some level trivializing what we're doing here, as if it's about nothing but sexual attraction."

"Well, that's what I feel, and I wonder if that's what you feel. I hope so, but it scares me too. I think it would really scare me if I did succeed in seducing you, but that's what I really want."

"You'd have gotten what you want, but also you'd have destroyed me as your therapist at the same time. You would both gain me but lose me."

"I know. So I think, what's the point of coming here if it's only going to be a frustrating situation no matter what?"

The therapist said, "It's as if you need to focus only on the narrow band of sexual feelings, as you imagine my response to you, rather than to permit in your imagination a wider range of feelings and thoughts that I could have toward you, or you toward me."

"I don't really know what you think of me. I don't think that I'm so extraordinary. I imagine lots of women do this with you."

It seemed to the therapist that, while the patient did in fact "know" what reaction her behaviors and words were intended to produce, she nevertheless was needing to disavow this fantasy of really impacting him, at the cost of diminishing her assessment of her own powers. He said, "Well, do you notice how you're putting yourself down, saying that you're not extraordinary? It's as if you don't want to think that you could be uniquely appealing, that you could be powerful, that you could have powerful effects on me, including emotionally." Not to join the patient in denial, realizing what was "really happening" between them, he chose to make use of his feelings to address this interpersonal reality as dealt with in her mind, i.e., as she both elaborated while defending against her fantasy of affecting him. Yet, he worried that he was skating dangerously close to the edge of admitting his own feelings, which would have constituted a gross enactment, from his point of view.

"I just don't think so," she replied. The patient continued to talk, mildly joking about using the therapy only for entertainment and pleasure, since she did not have any other source or outlet for that in her life, and why should she come here just for that? The therapist, having interpreted her diminution of the value of therapy, in addition to her diminution of herself, also noticed that she was very much diminishing him. As he looked at her across the room, he noticed as if for the first time, though in fact this was her typical posture, how she reclined in the chair languidly, reflecting upon her desires calmly, without pressure nor impulsivity in her speech, nor defensiveness, but utterly relaxed, confident in her right to her thoughts and feelings, and in her safety. Of course, wasn't this how a patient should be able to feel in therapy? He suddenly had a vision of her as being very powerful, in effect, casually using him as a sexual object, the way that she'd long described men using women.

The therapist then said, "I wonder if your self-dismissal, the way you present yourself as meek, unattractive, and helpless in your life and with me, could be a way to avoid feelings of being very powerful. It's as if you don't want to let yourself imagine that you could get what you want, that you could have that kind of impact on me, because it would frighten you to think of yourself as being powerful and at an advantage that way." The patient said, "I just can't see myself that way."

Several months later, she began for the first time in several years a dating relationship with a man. After a summer break from therapy, she began her first session back as follows: "While I was away, I worried that X (her boyfriend) was losing interest in me, but once I got back, I thought that I was losing interest in him. Actually, I missed you more than I missed him." There followed a pause.

The therapist asked, "How do you mean?"

"Well, I've already said what I was thinking. I don't want to get into all of that again. . . ."

"Even though you're having the thought, you feel you shouldn't say it, because you spoke about it before?"

"Well, I had a dream last night in which I gave you a gift, and you accepted it. It made me very happy. The dream wasn't specific about what the gift was. I do feel I'd like to give you something, to make this more equal. I think the gift I'd like to give you is listening to you telling me about *your* thoughts and feelings. Because that's what you give me. The relationship seems so one-sided; there is an air of unreality to it. Of course, maybe you're telling me your feelings would be a gift more to me than to you."

"The single act, my being open, telling you my thoughts and feelings, and your listening, would be a gift simultaneously, me to you, and you to me."

The patient laughed gently and said, "Yes, it would. I'd like that, because I feel that I can't give you anything, and I want to, to show my appreciation."

"For some reason you can't think or feel that you're giving me something by telling me what's on your mind?"

"I don't feel that it's worth much. If you were open with me, then we would be really friends. Maybe that's not how it's supposed to be. It can never happen, so I shouldn't think about it."

"Evidently, you are feeling friendly toward me, but you don't feel that pursuing that, talking about it, is allowed."

"I know you're not supposed to tell me how you feel, but I take that as saying that I'm not worthy of hearing. Even though I can guess how you might feel, I might be wrong."

"How do you mean?"

"How do I know, if you don't confirm my guesses? If I presumed I was guessing correctly that you like me, or even love me, and were mistaken, then I'd feel stupid and rejected."

"It sounds like you feel you can't let yourself go, imagining my thoughts and feelings about you, for fear that I'll disabuse you of your fantasies and tell you you're wrong."

"I think that you do like me, but I still want to hear it from you."

Over the next two years, the patient gradually admitted not so much frustration, but more sadness, that she could never have her wishes fulfilled with the therapist, even though she felt it a very real possibility that he loved her and might wish for the same fulfillment with her. The therapist never came verbally closer to admitting any feelings about her than illustrated above. Her sadness at times alternated with anger at him for his "bourgeois decency", but she at all times maintained the reality-perception that those limits were imposed by professional necessity. "I know it's supposedly in my own best interests, but why can't I get a chance to argue with those who write the rules?" As she experienced these feelings regarding the therapist, spontaneous associations and memories revived longings and disappointments she'd suffered in her relationship to her father. The therapist was able to interpret directly that with him, she was both re-experiencing what she'd felt over and over again with father's disappearances from her life, and also was trying to undo and correct that loss. She was seeking revenge on her father in effigy, by tormenting the therapist with tempting love he could not have. In being so compellingly seductive, she was expressing an identification with her father and his power, imagining that the therapist would be left awe-struck and helpless, as she'd been as a little girl. Turning a passive experience into an active one, she would reverse the roles. He would suffer what she had suffered.

She also reconnected with the grieving she had left incomplete by "just giving up" on her father, as she tearfully admitted her sorrow that she would eventually lose the therapist too. In time she felt that the expense of therapy was outweighing the benefit she was obtaining, given that she could never have what she "really wanted". Gradually "outgrowing" her need for self-negation when she expressed her wishes directly, she increasingly permitted herself to take on more ambitious projects at work, by which she rose in responsibility and position. She also got involved in a relationship with a man who was nonthreatening to her, with whom she could get what she wanted in reality, and they became engaged to be married. She terminated the therapy soon thereafter.

AFTERWORD

While the therapist treating this patient understood what was going on from both the "new" and "old" perspectives, he followed the classical model in his technique. That is, while noting his internal reactions to the patient's transference, his countertransference feelings, fantasies, and the pressure to act according to the patient's needs and wishes, he did not reveal or discuss them, but, within himself, used them as a guide in trying to understand what was going on within the patient and between the two of them. In his comments, he kept the focus on the patient's intrapsychic reality, including her ability to acknowledge and her need to deny her fantasies and guesses about the therapist's mental life in response to her. Though there was no overt enactment, one might argue that his "skating close to the edge" of self-revelation constituted a subtle enactment within appropriate technique.

Clearly, this was analytically oriented psychotherapy, in that transference took center stage explicitly for much of each session, from rather early in the treatment. One might ask how the patient, at only once-per-week therapy, was able to experience intense transference feelings so directly. Such an ability generally is more characteristic of borderline than neurotic patients, yet this patient was clearly in the healthy to neurotic grouping. How this patient acquired such an ability is unclear, but it probably related to a number of factors, such as a childhood characterized by seductiveness and then abandonment by a charismatic father, a lifelong ability to experience and verbalize affects, a hysterical personality style, an open and nonthreatening therapist, and much work between patient and therapist regarding resistances.

In summary, the patient developed a very intense and loving transference. At first feeling rebuffed by the therapist, she acted out her anger by quitting the therapy. When she returned, the therapist helped her see more clearly various transference meanings that had motivated her need to leave. There followed an intensification of erotic feelings in which she acted very seductively, powerfully forcing the therapist to deal with sexual temptation. He made decisive use of his countertransference feelings, without directly admitting them to the patient. He realized through his own inner reactions that she was exerting great power over him, implicitly reducing him to the helpless object of her desire, taking vengeance upon him as she had unconsciously wished but never had upon the father. His interpretation of her "making the therapy into a pornography show" and of her maintaining the outer presentation of herself as meek and helpless in order to keep herself from acknowledging that she could be powerful with him, preceded her starting a dating relationship with a man outside of therapy. We might infer that the insight imparted by this interpretation, together with other analogous interventions, caused a shift within her so that she could reduce her need to diminish herself, and instead could allow herself more consciously, directly, and effectively to acknowledge and express her powers. She shifted her attention to some extent from the therapist, but relinquished her hopes for fulfillment with him only gradually. In the process, she experienced and expressed increasingly differentiated tenderness and concern, as she grieved the losses of both her father and the therapist.

Chapter Ten

Mr. B and Ms. G:
Dynamically Oriented Psychotherapy

In this chapter we present two cases of dynamically oriented psychotherapy, one using the old model of transference and the other the new. Both cases seemed quite successful while they lasted, yet both ended precipitously and prematurely. Commentary about possible reasons for these unfortunate endings, in addition to other aspects of the cases, is included.

MR. B: DYNAMICALLY ORIENTED PSYCHOTHERAPY IN THE OLD MODEL

Mr. B, a 56-year-old man, married but distant from his wife for some time, working as an economist, the head of a division. He came to therapy because of escalating problems with paranoid thinking, intermittently controlled by medication in the past. He had not been on medication for several years and had never been in psychotherapy. Mr. B felt that he suffered greatly from a tragic childhood, which colored all aspects of his life. He further believed that he could benefit from talking about his past and desired psychotherapy.

Mr. B was placed on medication, and his paranoid thinking rapidly resolved. He undertook the psychotherapy with enthusiasm, talking easily and spontaneously. Sessions were twice weekly, and Mr. B was always early and eager to talk. In fact, he talked nonstop, from start to finish. His attitude always was very positive, and he rapidly felt relief from talking. As therapy progressed, he noted improvements in relations with his wife, his colleagues, and his boss. Not a week went by that Mr. B didn't tell me how much he valued the therapy, described as one of the highlights of his life. He felt relieved that he was finally able to talk about issues that he had neglected for so long.

Noting that Mr. B had a history of strained relations with colleagues and supervisors, related to a childhood of continual criticism and rejection by his father, I, on a number of occasions, brought up the possibility of an analogous difficulty occurring in the therapy hours with me. I noted that I was happy that Mr. B felt so positive toward me and the therapy, but because of his history, I just wanted to caution him that negative feelings could occur. If they were to occur, I hoped Mr. B would be able to talk readily about them with me. Mr. B noted his tendency from the past in this regard, but assured me that he only felt positively to me. The above was the extent of direct talk about the relationship between Mr. B and myself in the hours. There was a clearly positive, somewhat idealized transference always present, but only discussed as indicated above. Aided by this positive transference, and with a seemingly strong working alliance between the two of us, Mr. B went forward in talking about his life. Thus the treatment took the form of a dynamically oriented psychotherapy.

Initially, and for a number of months, Mr. B focused on his past life, discussing details of a very difficult childhood, where both parents seemed unattuned to Mr. B's needs and desires. Mr. B was viewed as someone to meet his parents' needs, as an extension of them rather than as a separate person. His parents' needs involved pretending that everything was fine, no matter what. There was to be no recognition of anything negative. Mr. B's parents talked little to each other and little their son, who was expected to mimic their view that everything was fine. Mr. B did comply with this expectation of overt and global denial, but with confusion and inner turmoil. One focus of the denial was on his mother's depression; her depression and suicide attempts were never mentioned or acknowledged. When she was away at the hospital, Mr. B was simply told that she would be back soon; when she returned, she acted as if she had never left. This atmosphere influenced Mr. B to become very anxious about any separations from his mother. He began to feel that maybe he had something to do with his mother's behavior. Maybe mother left when he misbehaved; maybe she was punishing him. He began to have vague and ill defined thoughts of some plot or conspiracy that might help explain her mysterious disappearances and reappearances. In the absence of any explanations, Mr. B comforted himself with his own thoughts here, which gradually became somewhat delusional in quality.

Sessions focused almost exclusively on clarifying and elaborating what transpired in Mr. B's childhood, with numerous dynamic hypotheses put forward to help understand that very difficult time. Mr. B acted as if he couldn't believe what had happened in his childhood. He was mystified and perplexed. "How could his father treat him that way? Did he know nothing about how to raise a kid?" I basically listened to Mr. B, shared in his amazement, confirmed some of his hypotheses, and offered alternative perspectives. Later I helped Mr. B correlate his childhood with some of his later paranoid ideas and with his later difficulties of relating to others.

The following exchange was typical of the sessions:

Mr. B: You know, I don't think that my father ever told me he liked me. He never comforted me, and he never shared anything about what was happening with my mother. It was just amazing. How could he have treated me that way? And my mother didn't act much differently, although it was clear that she liked me. I just don't understand how parents could treat their child that way. They must have been really ignorant about bringing up a child. I never expressed my needs, so maybe they assumed I didn't have any. I know my mother was depressed, but I just don't understand it. Do you think that she was so involved with her depression that she was oblivious to me?

Therapist: Yes, that is quite possible. Your mother was very involved in hiding her depression, and your father in efforts in dealing with her, so that they neglected you. You were very attuned to your parents' needs and desires. You knew they wanted to ignore the problems and pretend that all was well, so you didn't ask what was going on, or show that you were bothered. You did what they wished, but you suffered inwardly. Your parents were unattuned to your suffering and to your needs as an individual separate from them. Neither treated you as a person with your own needs. Possibly you contributed here by going along with their denial.

Patient: It's just amazing. How could they do that? Did they not have anyone to tell them how to act as a parent? Actually when I think about it, I think that my father never had reasonable parenting from his own father. I don't think that my father ever mentioned his own father to me when I was a kid. . . .

Months were spent in this way, with Mr. B focusing on his childhood and being amazed at the poor treatment by his parents. Very gradually he began to view aspects of his early life in alternative ways, acquiring some "understanding" of what his parents might have been experiencing, including factors that might have contributed to their neglect of him. Additionally, he began to understand his contribution to their neglect. Concomitantly, he began to feel more comfortable with his parents and his past. Sessions always took the form of a collaborative effort between Mr. B and myself, each of us listening to the other's ideas, and jointly arriving at various hypotheses. There was always a spirit of cooperation, with the two of us working together, with the common goal of clarifying, elaborating, and understanding Mr. B's past. Again there was little focus on Mr. B's relation to me.

After months of almost exclusive focus on his childhood, Mr. B began to expand his thinking, with attempts to understand how his childhood influenced and caused difficulties later in life. He focused on his tendency, in any ambiguous situation, to feel criticized by others, to feel that others might be against him, and to withdraw in these circumstances. He focused also on his tendency to discount his own ideas and feelings and to respond to others in ways he felt would please them, in a similar manner to how he related to his parents. There was specific focus on the negative consequences of these tendencies, including the loss of several relationships and the loss of a job. Mr. B maintained a sense of enthusiasm in understanding these things. The collaborative relationship between the two of us continued, and Mr. B furthered his understanding. With this expanded focus in these sessions, Mr. B began to report better relations in his current life, both at work and at home. A sample exchange, somewhat similar to the first reported exchange, is as follows:

> *Mr. B:* You know what I think? I think that all those years, when my parents didn't talk to me, when they acted as if everything was all right, and when I pretended to think the same way, had their toll. I think I learned to act that way with my parents, then began to act that way with everyone else. It's hard to believe, but I really think that this was the case. What do you think?

> *Therapist:* I can't help but agree with you. Today, in a similar way that you acted with your parents, you tap into what other people want from you and respond in accordance with that. You do that sometimes without realizing it, as if you're not conscious of what you're doing.

> *Patient:* It's hard to believe. That's exactly what happened last week at work. I was really worried that my boss was critical of me and didn't like me, so I said what I thought he wanted to hear. It worked out okay, except that I didn't feel so good.

With the knowledge that therapy with Mr. G ended somewhat precipitously and unexpectedly, about which I will elaborate shortly, I do want to reiterate at this point, that I continued throughout the therapy, whenever there was an "opening," to hint at possibilities of Mr. B feeling negatively to me, in ways analogous to what he described of his relations with others. Whenever this was mentioned, Mr. B assured me that all was positive between us. The therapy lasted almost a year, always twice weekly, in the format as presented. Again, Mr. B and I maintained a mutually positive and collaborative relationship, with a good working alliance, with the joint task of looking at, clarifying, and understanding Mr. B's childhood, and seeing how it contributed to Mr. B's early problems. The difficulties and problems of early life were then correlated with more recent problems. A positive transference with some idealization always was overt. Thus the therapy was very much one of a dynamic orientation. The transference was clearly present, yet never the center of focus. Mr. B, via a positive working alliance and a uniformly positive (and somewhat idealized) transference, was able to explore and understand his childhood, then to correlate his childhood with his later life. Concomitantly, he increasingly felt better about himself and his life. It might also be noted that the therapy was in accordance with the old model. Anonymity, abstinence, and relative neutrality were maintained, not so much by intent, but because the therapy naturally unfolded that way.

The fact that the treatment ended a bit prematurely remains somewhat confusing to me. One day Mr. B came in and said that he felt totally better and was ready to leave. He thought he had little more to say, at least not now, and that he had met his goals. Again he thanked me profusely, reiterating that the therapy with me was one of the great experiences of his life. Feeling surprised, if not shocked, I could not help but wonder if Mr. B was stopping a bit precipitously and if other factors (in addition to the success of the therapy) might be operative. After Mr. B rapidly assured me that all was well, I agreed with him about his progress, but still wondered if it might be a bit premature to stop now. I offered several reasons as to why Mr. B might want to stay, including consolidating his gains and continuing to actively explore how his past was influencing current relationships. I also wondered if some time spent on discussing termination itself might be useful. Mr. B agreed that these were worthy causes, yet was adamant about stopping now. Sensing Mr. B's pressure and defensiveness, I did not push his continuing, feeling that it would be important to end on a positive note, leaving the door open for Mr. B to continue later. Thus, I briefly reviewed the therapy and Mr. B's gains, and a seemingly successful therapy ended precipitously.

To repeat once again, the model for the therapy was clearly that of a dynamically oriented one. It is not that the transference was absent nor played a small role. In contrast, the transference was markedly there, contributing to an idealized atmosphere and a positive working alliance. The transference, in fact, was most probably responsible for Mr. B's premature termination, although I cannot say exactly how. To oversimplify, Mr. B either became too anxious about (unconscious) positive feelings to me, or he ran from negative feelings (fearful or paranoid) that were beginning to emerge (most probably on an unconscious level). Thus the transference was probably crucial in both the success of the therapy and in its "premature" ending. Despite its importance, there was minimal discussion and focus on the transference.

One might ask the question whether there should have been more focus and more persistent efforts to focus on Mr. B's relation to me, with the hope that more discussion would have inhibited Mr. B from terminating. Actually I tried, whenever I could, to add this focus, yet Mr. B was not prepared nor able to do this. I might be wrong, but I do not think it would have been useful or even possible to push talking about the relationship more. Mr. B had his own agenda, knew what he wanted to pursue, and did that diligently and successfully while he remained in treatment.

MS. G: DYNAMICALLY ORIENTED PSYCHOTHERAPY IN THE NEW MODEL

Ms. G, a 38-year-old professional woman, was referred to me by her psychotherapist of four years, after a very serious suicide attempt. Ms. G, upon awakening the next day, expressed great regret that she was still alive. Her therapist, having tried her best in every way possible to help Ms. G prevent such an occurrence, felt sufficiently upset and betrayed by Ms. G, who violated a clearly agreed upon "no suicide" pact, and thus the referral to me. Ms. G readily agreed to see me, although she voiced great skepticism about the value of therapy. She also readily agreed to meet twice weekly, in contrast to her weekly sessions with her previous therapist. It is noteworthy that she expressed little regret about leaving her past therapist, for whom she showed few feelings. This stance continued throughout the year of therapy with me.

Ms. G remained skeptical and ambivalent throughout her year of therapy. Despite this stance, she came to all sessions, was virtually never late, and in fact had a tendency to arrive very early. The therapy had a marked educational component, characterized by Ms. G asking me various questions about life and living, and then comparing my way of thinking to her own. She was particularly interested in the differences in our thinking, wondering whether she thought rationally or not. A working alliance was rapidly established, with one clear joint goal of trying to understand Ms. G's ways of thinking, especially as related to suicide. This goal was pursued with little overt focus on the transference. Countertransferentially, I liked Ms. G very much and felt a great desire to help. A mild overprotective attitude was noted by myself. Ms. G was pleasant, even charming, and very cooperative. In fact, it seemed that being cooperative, being pleasant, and doing what "she was supposed to do" were life-long traits that Ms. G had acquired in a somewhat fanatical way. These traits contributed to an "as if" quality to her and to a lack of feeling and emotion.

There were two main themes in the year of therapy. The first was Ms. G's idea that it was totally reasonable to both think about killing herself and in fact doing that if she so desired. She saw no reason to think otherwise. Life did not seem so significant or pleasurable, so why not have the option of ending it? In fact, given her life-long pattern of being totally compliant, she felt that she deserved the option of varying from that compliance in this one way. Exploration here focused on her relationship with her parents, her always doing what was expected, to the extent that she would conceal any feelings or ideas that she thought her parents might find objectionable. Related to the above was a time in childhood when Ms. G's mother was in danger of dying, and when Ms. G. vowed to be the "best daughter in the world" if her mother lived. Ms. G, in fact, was living up to this promise. The possibility of resentment and anger about her life-long compliance, and the relationship of this compliance to her sense of entitlement in refusing to comply in the most important way, was discussed but not well understood.

Regarding her thinking about suicide (that it was reasonable to kill herself if she so desired), Ms. G was interested in my alternative perspectives, yet very resistant to changing her thinking. When I noted that very few people thought as she did, she would say to me, "Really?" Then the next session, she would tell me that she had "checked it out" with several friends, and "yes, I was correct." She had little sympathy, however, for one of my favorite ideas, that thinking in general was very changeable; could greatly vary from day-to-day or month-to-month; and, in fact, was highly related to one's moods, which also could vary greatly depending on such factors as the events of the day, changes in the environment, and one's internal world. Thus, although someone (i.e., Ms. G) might feel one day that she might like to die, this feeling could be totally reversed in a short period of time. I made statements such as the above in many altered forms and ways: Ms. G most always responded that despite all that I said, she had yet to experience life as all that great. It is worth mentioning that Ms. G maintained her opinions despite a number of clear positives in her life, including many friends, an excellent job, high intelligence, and being a very attractive young woman. Although Ms. G maintained her opinions, she seemed to enjoy talking to me about my alternative ideas. She gradually began to give the impression that she might be changing her thinking, if ever so slightly.

The other main theme in the therapy was the attempt to correlate Ms. G's negative thinking with mood fluctuations, sometimes difficult to discern, that related to external events. Ms. G, in fact, was influenced by external events but often had great difficulty in experiencing, identifying, and differentiating her feelings. At times of particular stress, Ms. G experienced a terrible "crappy" feeling, like a feeling of emptiness or nothingness. When these horribly painful feelings became intense, Ms. G would respond in several ways: by heightened exercise, by work, by complete withdrawal (lying in bed for hours), and sometimes by acute suicidal ideation. Much time in the therapy was spent focusing on these painful states and correlating them with events, usually of rejection or betrayal. Within the undifferentiated "crappy" feelings,

Ms. G was able to find a number of separate feelings: anger, rage, shame, humiliation, and sadness. She began to be able to differentiate these different feelings and to correlate them to her internal and external world.

Throughout the therapy, there appeared to be a reasonable working alliance, joint goals, interesting conversation, and a lot of give-and-take. This alliance seemed to gradually strengthen, although this strengthening was not always obvious. The content of the sessions went back and forth from the two main themes, to Ms. G's day-to-day events, to her current relationship with her friends and family, and to her childhood. Left out in this otherwise rather fluid exchange were any feelings or thoughts about me. Ms. G obviously viewed me in a consciously positive way, as a mentor, as a benign parent, working with her to help her achieve her goals. Yet, this was largely not articulated. Thus the therapy was clearly of a dynamically oriented modality. As I was exceptionally open to sharing my views, although always focused on Ms. G and her questions, the therapy was operating in accordance with the new model, as described in this book.

Therapy with Ms. G came to an abrupt end, after a two-week vacation by me. Interestingly enough, I thought it would be advantageous to focus more on the transference, and that this focus would be enhanced by increased sessions. Actually, I was hopeful that Ms. G would take me up on this offer and was excited about the possibility of changing to a more analytically oriented model. Yet this change never happened. When I returned from my vacation, there was a message from Ms. G stating that she was ending the therapy. When I called her, she politely informed me that she was feeling better, had several important decisions regarding her career about which she needed to focus, and wanted a break from therapy. Ms. G was totally negative to the idea of coming in to talk about her decision, nor did she agree with my idea that the therapy might be useful to her work-related decision making. She totally opposed my idea of her discussing her ideas of stopping therapy with one of her close friends. Ms. G had already discussed her resentment of her mother's intrusiveness and overbearingness and I certainly did not want to create an analogous situation. So despite my great misgivings about her abrupt termination, I only added that I did think that more therapy would be useful, and that I would be available whenever she wanted to resume. Thus ended the therapy with Ms. G.

It was rather clear that over my vacation, Ms. G had altered her thinking about therapy. Influenced by my absence, she changed her stance from ambivalently positive to clearly negative. Discussing this change in thinking might have been useful, but it was impossible without further sessions. I might also mention that possible ramifications of my vacation break for Ms. G had been discussed at some length. Additionally, the availability of a substitute therapist was proposed and discussed. Ms. G did not desire to see someone in my absence and insisted that she would be fine.

COMPARISON OF MR. B TO MS. G

It might be of use to examine the similarities in the therapies of Ms. G and Mr. B. Both therapies were clearly of the dynamically oriented modality. With Ms. G, the therapy proceeded in accordance with the new model; with Mr. B it was more in accordance with the old model. Of clear relevance was that neither therapy included much discussion of the transference. Mr. B continually commented on the value of the therapy but never voiced more complicated feelings. Despite numerous efforts to engage him further in this regard, Mr. B was not responsive. Ms. G voiced much more ambivalence about the therapy, yet appeared to be working in a positive way. Little effort was made to engage her in a more transferential manner, because she did not appear to be experiencing her feelings in ways that could be easily verbalized. Both Ms. G and Mr. B made excellent use of the sessions, yet both therapies ended precipitously and unexpectedly. One could make the case that both ended because of transference feelings that, if verbalized, could have helped extend the treatment. Yet neither patient seemed able to become more overtly involved in a discussion of the transference. Of the two, termination with Ms. G was more worrisome, because of her history of suicidal tendencies. Despite a relatively good year of therapy, Ms. G would need considerable more treatment to overcome those tendencies. Mr. B was less worrisome. Despite the short length of his therapy, he was able to make changes that were potentially more permanent. Additionally, an intensification of symptoms on his part would not be so disturbing. In fact, it is reasonable to think that given an intensification, he would return to treatment.

A final note regarding the transference on these two cases of dynamically oriented psychotherapy is in order. When we speak about the transference with Mr. B and Ms. G (and the lack of its overt expression), we are clearly referring to the object-related aspects of the transference, termed the representational dimension by Lachmann (2000) in Chapter 2. Regarding the selfobject dimension of the transference, this was clearly operative and important with both these patients. To varying degrees, with both Mr. B and Ms. G, the therapeutic relationship provided such important selfobject needs as self-cohesion, increased self esteem, comforting and soothing, validation, and vitality. With Ms. G (and possibly with Mr. B), it is likely that a rupture in the selfobject dimension contributed to the premature termination. With

Ms. G, this was overt, when she began to think very differently about the therapeutic relationship in my absence (when on vacation). Dynamically oriented psychotherapy, distinguished by its lack of overt focus on the object-related aspects of the transference, is however often characterized by the clear manifestation of the selfobject dimensions of the transference.

Chapter Eleven

A Very Classical Case of
Analytically Oriented Psychotherapy

In the following case, the therapist conducted psychotherapy in as close a way as possible to classical psychoanalysis. Thus, this case is one of analytically oriented psychotherapy in the strictest sense, with the therapist believing most literally in the "old model" of transference.

The therapist maintained a very conservative stance, keeping his own personal countertransferential feelings almost completely absent from his report. As he wrote to the authors of this book, he saw his "minimally cathected" reactions to the patient as clues indicative primarily about the patient. He described his therapeutic approach as one keeping primarily to addressing the patient's resistances and defenses and clarifying what came up in the patient's thoughts, only interpreting when the material was very vivid and full of affect. He felt that his abstinence, neutrality, and anonymity ultimately permitted a deeper transference experience to develop, with greater mobilization of the patient's underlying conflicts, and with greater "shifting of his pathological character structure" than would have been possible had he chosen to gratify the patient's various demands for a "more personal relationship."

A male elementary school teacher about thirty years old came to treatment complaining that he "always worries" and feeling perpetually unsatisfied with his job. Despite ability and diligence, he felt he had never met his functional and income potential. He met the criteria for compulsive personality, complaining especially of difficulties dealing with or expressing emotions. He suffered from indecisiveness, self-doubt, avoidance of competition, procrastination, and overriding dependency, especially on his parents and on his wife. He also had a phobia of air travel that he felt inhibited his prospects for any career change and frustrated his family's wish for adventurous vacations. He had a school phobia in the third grade, manifested by frequent absences for "not feeling well." His father, a businessman, was often preoccupied with work and thus showed little interest in the children. The patient remembered little overt warmth or encouragement from his father, only the exhortation to "try harder." His mother was a doting housewife. He had little sexual experience prior to his marriage at age 29 to a woman especially approved by his parents.

OPENING PHASE

In the first session of twice a week analytically oriented psychotherapy, the patient said, "I've heard that in therapy one goes back to early childhood memories. So I tried to think about what my earliest memory was. This is what I came up with: I was sitting on my mother's lap in the car, leaning my head against her breast. She seemed irritable, told me that I was hurting her, and took me off her lap to sit away from her. . . ." It seemed to the therapist that the patient was offering this as a "gift", in an unconscious attempt to show his compliance and perhaps to decrease the possibility for competitive aggression arising between them. In the earliest sessions, the patient expressed his expectation that the therapist had some superior wisdom, saying, "I imagine you've heard all this before." At first always genial, he anticipated that what he said would be "tied up neatly" into a "deep interpretation." He saw his role as that of the passive recipient, the therapist as the benevolent provider.

Over the first month or two, as the wished-for powerful interpretation did not materialize, the patient began increasingly to express doubts as to the worth or relevance of his thoughts and became increasingly silent. To the therapist's inquiries, he replied that what occurred in his mind seemed "not connected to anything," "not leading anywhere," or "too superficial." The therapist made such reflective comment as, "You feel you have to see how it is important before you can say what you're thinking." Many such interactions over the early months served gradually to demonstrate to the patient that his prejudging the value or relevance of what occurred to him caused him to omit many thoughts that would be difficult for him to say. As his threshold for speaking lowered, it emerged that in his silences, he was worrying, "What does he [the therapist] think of me?" or, "I feel stupid," or, "I wish he'd help out." Only in time did there emerge more clear resentment at being left "too much on my own," but he would preface anything that could possibly be construed as a complaint with such comments as, "I'm sure you must have good reasons for what you're doing."

We thus observe that the patient's developing relationship to the therapist had begun to interfere with the treatment, despite his wish to comply. He was seeing the therapist as someone powerful; his assumption that the therapist was also benevolent apparently served to defend against an opposite fear, perhaps that he could be negligent, critical or abusive. Notice how the patient saw his difficulty proceeding as the result of his own deficiencies, an attack on himself. He also was "sure" the therapist had "good reasons". We might call this a defensive "reaction formation", seeing the therapist only in a rosy light. These attitudes toward himself and the therapist seemed unconsciously designed to weaken any potential demands or criticisms he might have of the therapist, and to prevent his becoming too aware of dissatisfied or angry feelings. They also would preempt the criticism he feared from the therapist and would serve to prevent hostility between them.

The therapist preferred that the fully elaborated transference fantasies and feelings emerge spontaneously. He therefore focused his interventions at this point only on intrapsychic defense mechanisms interfering with this development and did not address the interpersonal dimension. For example, he might at a particular time draw the patient's attention to how his difficulty proceeding seemed to result from a specific concern, for example, that he might be criticized for "inadequate performance". The patient's coming to recognize this would constitute a "working through" of that momentary defense, as indicated by the emergence of further associations and material which until then had remained latent. The therapist feared that to address the transference more directly at this point would have tended to dampen the feelings and promote mere intellectualization, while he hoped that clarifying for the patient his resistances would permit the transference to ripen, making the experience more real.

Where earlier of his parents, he had only said, "They did what they thought best," by the fourth or fifth month, the patient began gradually to confess disappointment in them and was surprised at one point to realize that he had been deriding his father. He continued to treat the therapist with great deference, but referred to his internist (to whom he was going for gastrointestinal complaints) as follows: "I never know if he remembers what I told him last time, or if I have to remind him all over again. He seems to have his own pre-set ideas about what's wrong, but I don't think he's telling me the worst. He doesn't seem to take my questions seriously and he is patronizing. Everybody questions his competence." At this, the therapist wondered if the patient might have any similar doubts about him. The patient laughed and replied, "As I was talking, I had the thought that you might think that. But no, I really don't think that way about you. I do see how you could construct a parallel, intellectually."

We note that the patient in effect gave an affirmative response to the therapist's inquiry. He had "had the thought" but immediately experienced it in the form of one "you might think." That is, he accomplished a disavowal by automatically, without being aware of doing so, utilizing the defensive operation of projection. He further dismissed any possible emotional significance by intellectualizing about "how you could construct a parallel." We might suspect that, in fact, the patient was expressing his feelings about the therapist exactly, but needed unconsciously to disguise this expression in the displacement to the figure of the internist, a "transference allusion." This would serve to help him maintain his consciously deferential attitude toward the therapist, again, to deny the possibility of hostile or critical feelings coming up within him toward this male authority figure directly.

The patient at first also portrayed his wife in an idealized fashion, as not suffering from inhibitions and anxieties such as he did, but as having much greater functional capacities. He permitted her also to act as an authority for him. "My wife will tell me if I'm drinking too much. She knows when enough is enough. . . . She gives me permission. I use her as a barometer." Similarly, he used her as a voice-piece for sentiments he was apparently unable to express himself, for example, complaints about the expense of therapy. He seemed reticent to distinguish his own feelings from hers, and would speak of "we," as in, "We feel that . . . ," even if at other times he had expressed a countervailing feeling.

For example, he said, "I really don't care if we get a new house right away, but I go along with it because it's important to her. But that makes the therapy harder to continue to afford. She's giving me a hard time about coming here."

The therapist asked, "Do you say you don't care about getting the house, because it would be difficult for you to admit that you really do want a new house? It might feel unacceptable for you to emphasize your own needs."

The patient said, "Well, I wouldn't mind getting one!" The therapist went on to ask if he quoted his wife's dissatisfaction because it would be difficult for him to acknowledge that he had concerns himself about the expense of the therapy. To this, the patient replied, "Sometimes, I do worry about the expense, what we're giving up so I can do this." Thus, the therapist's addressing the patient's defensive disavowal (of desires for better things, then of transference resentments, which he instead attributed to his wife) permitted the patient to move more to acknowledging wishes and feelings as his own.

We have seen how the patient tended to project a sense of competence and strength onto certain others, whom he regarded as authority figures, in order to maintain a gratifying passive dependence. He could not yet permit himself to acknowledge such attributes of strength in himself. The therapist pointed out how the patient felt in a dilemma: he was relying upon the therapy for help in overcoming his inhibitions and low self-esteem, yet he was also having resentments against the therapist, that he felt he shouldn't express too directly.

The patient fretted about his lower earning power, less than his wife's. With their small house and old cars, he felt he could not get ahead, and he persisted in blaming this in part upon the expense of the therapy, even when assured of a high rate of insurance reimbursement. "Money's tight. T. [his wife] is tired of it, and I'm tired of it . . . I feel like a monkey running around after the peanuts that someone is throwing on the floor. . . . It gives me an excuse to be stingy." Thus, in response to the therapist's addressing the patient's need for specific defenses, there more clearly was emerging an aspect of what had been defended against, the patient's resentment of the therapy. While the therapist sat back in his "easy chair," the patient felt that he did all the work, but that he benefitted little. He relied on hoarding as a regressive but more consciously acceptable solution, hoping that this would make him feel better about himself. What was still difficult to acknowledge, the more directly self-assertive feelings, he turned to acting out unconsciously.

ACTING OUT IN THE TRANSFERENCE NEUROSIS

At about a year and a half into the treatment, having accrued a standing debt to the therapist, the patient revealed that, allegedly unaware, he'd spent over two thousand dollars of insurance reimbursements intended for the therapy. He nevertheless avoided discussing this. In a bland manner, he planned other large expenditures, including a pension fund, and told of his wife's "taking $200 off the top" of her biweekly paycheck for a separate account ("It's no big deal"), without seeing any connection to his debt to the therapist. He complained of always having been in "a fog about figures," unable to "put things together." He seemed to have an hysterical blindness or paralysis of cognition and maintained a bland indifference. When by a further miscalculation he during this period again underpaid, he proposed simply to have the deficit increase; he'd repay it six months hence.

The therapist persistently pointed out how the patient kept domestic money matters isolated in his mind from the debt here, how he alternatively struggled with and sought to avoid the debt issue, how he wished to displace this conflict into the future, and how he was perhaps withholding some thoughts and information in the sessions, just as he was withholding the money. He wondered if the patient wasn't putting thoughts, feelings, or fantasies into actions instead of words, and said, "Perhaps by maintaining the debt you're seeking to maintain a certain kind of relationship with me."

There emerged memories of his father's "tightness," "rigidity," and closed-mouthedness about money. "I had to beg him to go sign for my first house loan, even though it wouldn't cost him anything." The patient remembered as a child "keeping the change" without his father's permission. One sign of working through the resistance appeared as he began offering transference interpretations of his own: "Maybe since I felt my father didn't give me much, I took what I thought he should have given me. Is it that I feel I don't get enough from you, so I take without asking? . . . Maybe I fear that if I pay the debt, I'd be in over my head and wouldn't be able to keep up." To pay the debt (or a full fee) threatened a closer relationship with the therapist and a therapy that would move along faster.

Thus, by the end of the second year, there had developed a powerful father-transference, now being relived and examined in the therapy. On the one hand, the patient felt that the therapist was a demanding taskmaster, seeking to extract what he could not give. The therapy seemed an overwhelming and exhausting drain on his resources. "I feel pulled. I'm tired, just tired. . . . I come here and I just get beat up." He sought to maintain a dependent, passive stance in the therapy, "like a kid," who would not need to be responsible or accountable. "It's true, I made a mistake, but I guess I have wished you'd tell me that I wouldn't have to pay it back." He wished to feel valuable about himself through getting the therapist's approval but expected to be disappointed. On the other hand, he apparently also felt stronger and safer if he could be in his father's role. As he became freer about this issue, he reflected, "Maybe there's a conflict between rebelling against all that tightness and rigidity, on the one hand, and trying to retain it, on the other. Maybe I feel like my father was right to be that way." Thus, he treated the therapist as his father had treated him, feeling that he was torturing the therapist, or "pushing you to your limits," "cutting off your income." He thus was feeling deeply involved in an ambivalent negative-transference situation with the therapist as "father".

In one session, after a silence of several minutes, the patient said, "You know, I don't have any idea where this came from, but I just had a daydream. It's kind of embarrassing, but I guess I'll say it. Maybe it was triggered by the sound of tires screeching outside a minute ago. I imagined that I was coming to the office and there was a crowd gathered in the street. You'd been hit by a car, and were lying there, bleeding. You needed CPR. I was wondering if I were the only one who could do it, and was hesitating. That's it." The patient paused. The therapist asked, "That's it?" The patient then continued, "It's kind of weird, the idea of me saving your life and kissing you, well not kissing you—God, did I say that?—but having to breathe for you . . . it gives me the creeps."

This spontaneous daydream, even though elicited by association to a chance stimulus, appeared "at once", "whole", as if pre-formed. His reluctance to tell it (silence, embarrassment) inadvertently revealed some premonition of its latent, discomforting meaning. Disguised in the agency of the automobile accident, it revealed toward the therapist murderous wishes, while, disguised as resuscitative duty, it expressed wishes which were loving. He made further efforts to avoid recognizing its significance ("that's it"), but when meaning was revealed by a slip of the tongue, it evoked denial, astonishment, and a quantum of unpleasant affect. Thus, there were activated, in the intensified therapeutic process and transference, more freely appearing primitive fantasies and memories, associated with powerful affect.

Brief review of a somewhat later session will illustrate this further. Having begun the session talking about the "compliance-resistance cycle," as he called it, the patient recalled how as a child riding for the first time in an airplane (of which he as an adult had become quite phobic), he got "all worked up" with anxiety. For a while as a college student he also had a phobia about riding in trains, fearing that he might get stuck in a tunnel. "Both planes and trains are long things that go up and down, or in and out," he observed. He next noticed the ceiling lights in the office, which he thought looked like penises, and thought, "That's what happens to people who don't comply . . . I've heard about how people can fear castration, but never thought it applied to me. . . . So I've grown up trying to please everybody. . . . Maybe I thought that if I were bad as a kid, I'd be jerked around, maybe by my penis." He then became anxious that in the therapy he might "find out that I was sexually abused."

The idea of homosexuality was absolutely taboo, yet sexual attraction and activity with women was hardly ever mentioned, and when mentioned, weakly. He mentioned without complaint how he and his wife had sex infrequently, offering to one another usually somatic reasons: "We're both worn out." He was more involved with passive-aggressive and retentive struggles with the prohibiting father. In part this allowed him to avoid the forbidden sexual arena and its dangers. It seemed that he unconsciously anticipated that any sexual activity would be punished by the father, just as he saw the therapist as preventing his pleasure, wanting to take his money so that he could not buy a new car or bigger house. The therapist wondered if the patient felt that he was not permitted to talk about sex in the therapy. Instead, the patient spoke about feeling "drained," as if these were the consequences of masturbation. Life for him seemed to consist of frustration and disappointment. In his fantasies he aimed high and tried to be good, but received little gratification. "The school board treats us like peons." His phobias, his choice of profession, and his character all seemed to have derived from his choice (or necessity) to give up phallic assertiveness.

The day after the patient finally repaid the debt he reported one of his very rare dreams. He was riding in an airplane, and, "It was OK, there was no anxiety. . . . Maybe the therapy is like a plane ride." Saying they were "going to bite off a short plane trip," he planned to test the progress he had made in overcoming his phobia, thinking it would justify his wish to "wrap up" the therapy several months hence. He thus looked to external behavior as the means and criterion for cure.

TERMINATION AS A
RESISTANCE TO INTENSIFYING TRANSFERENCE

The more he realized the depth and intensity of his involvement in the therapy, the more this patient also spoke of his wish to leave. He complained of the expense, the "trip" (by auto), and his obligation to his wife, whom he quoted (in the service of his own resistance) as being "ready for me to finish here." He felt that giving to the therapy must be taking from his marriage. Even as he acknowledged that these were "probably not my real reasons for wanting to end the treatment," he nevertheless felt as if the therapist was coercing him into coming, refusing to grant the validity of his wishes and reasons for leaving. He continued to complain about being frustrated and disappointed at not getting from the therapist the kind of relationship and approving feedback he needed. He had never had a prolonged male friendship. The therapist interpreted, "You say you wish for a close relationship with a man, as with your father or with me. Yet you may flee the one here, because you fear that to stay would lead to a struggle in which you'd have to give up your will, or be trapped, or subjugated." It appeared to the therapist that the patient's fear of his wishes to remain in the therapy and the fantasized fulfillment of his wishes, originating in his relationship with his father, were driving him away.

In the next session, the patient spoke about how his anxiety about plane rides and about the therapy were similar. Then he said, "Could it be that I'm looking at our relationship as a substitute for what I never got from my dad?" He went on to remember how, if he would get ill in school, his father would carry him home in his arms. "The doctor would prescribe an enema." This was administered by his father, with some regularity. "I remember him holding me upside down on his lap and injecting the soapy water up there. I was supposed to hold it in as long as I could, until it hurt. Later, when I was 10 or 12, my mother did it." He noted that an airplane, a syringe, and a penis, are all "long things that move." He complained when the therapist pointed out resistance or a defense, with, "That feels like an enema to me." He admitted at times feeling sexually stimulated "by some of the things we discuss in here," and expressed the concern that he might discover he was homosexual. Having been overstimulated in childhood, he experienced the psychotherapeutic situation now as too stimulating.

The patient began to describe more active sexual attraction for some of the female teachers at the school where he worked. At the same time, he more insistently described his wife's impatience with the psychotherapy. This served again to camouflage his own reasons for needing to flee. He portrayed his wife as powerful and decisive, less compulsive, more competent and assertive than he. He claimed that she was jealous of his closeness to and time spent with the therapist. Having promised he would quit the therapy by the summer break (at the end of the third year), he felt he could not disappoint her and go back on his word. Thus, while he sought to escape the father-transference with the therapist, he was experiencing his wife also as a "father-figure." Helpless, dependent, feeling without a will of his own, he would be powerfully intruded upon by one or the other of them.

The therapist pointed out his feeling caught between his wife and the therapist; how difficult it must be to think of angering his wife, considering how much he relied on her; that leaving the therapy perhaps represented defying and frustrating the therapist, just as he may have wished to defy, frustrate, and leave his father; that intense unresolved conflicts with his father made him feel compelled to leave the treatment, as if something seemed very dangerous to him in the idea of remaining, but that the reasons were not at all fully clear.

All of this seemed only to increase a crescendo of excitement, with which the patient could deal only by solidifying his resolve. Apparently wanting the therapist to urge him to stay, he was getting the therapist to "do something to him." That is, he was provoking an intrusion that he experienced both as frightening, upsetting, and pleasurable. We can see that the therapist's insightful comments were having an effect quite independent of the intended, lexical content of the words spoken. Although experienced by the patient in part as informative, they were also experienced as the instruments by which his fearful fantasies about the father relationship were being realized. Thus, the therapeutic conversation, even when the therapist's interventions are correct and appropriate, may nevertheless become the medium for enactment.

Though he repeatedly asked the therapist to acknowledge his choice to leave as a legitimate, reasonable decision, it seemed to the therapist that his doing so would have confirmed the patient's passive masochistic self-image, by which "less should be enough for me." That is, the patient was in effect taking the position that a less than full resolution of his conflicts, resulting in less than thorough increase in phallic functioning, should have been acceptable. The therapist abstained from granting this wish to the patient, thinking that had he agreed, he would have finally proven to the patient, in accordance with his father, that the patient was not worth working with. The patient might also have been frightened of his potential aggression against a woman, his wife, who would interfere with his attempt to improve his life. Remaining in therapy thus seemed to threaten his marriage, upon which he felt dependent. He thus left at the end of the school year, expressing his gratitude to the therapist, and hoping, as he offered a farewell handshake, that the therapist would not hold it against him that they were parting in "gentlemen's disagreement."

AFTERWORD

The therapist in this case took a classic stance, remaining largely neutral, anonymous, abstinent, and "objective", in the sense that he saw himself as dealing with the patient's intrapsychic dynamics (e.g., his defense-impulse configurations) from a removed position, as if he were not himself involved or implicated. He would address the defenses and resistances as they appeared and "see what emerged." The therapist claimed that this stance permitted the emergence and elaboration of a most intense transference, very clearly representing and externalizing the patient's pre-existing, unconscious, highly conflictual internal object-relations structure: his passive-compliant, guiltily rebellious relation to his father.

Yet, the patient ultimately seemed unable to manage the intensity of the impulses, fearful fantasies, and affects brought out. One could argue that the therapist's professional stance itself became a stimulus for the very transference agenda that was supposedly to be nothing but something externalized. The therapist acted the role of objective "authority" (albeit a warm and concerned one), interpreting the patient's defenses and resistances as would a benign but uninvolved scientist analyzing a phenomenon in a clinical laboratory. To the patient, merely to listen to the pronouncements of such a therapist may have felt like being forced to submit to someone who was in fact in a superior position. Likewise, the therapist's abstinent stance, doing little more than making such interpretations, declining to grant the patient's wishes for more help or for more acknowledgement, might have been experienced by the patient as in fact expressing real stinginess. The therapist's never expressing or acknowledging anything of his own reactions might have constituted a real deprivation to this patient, who longed for a close friendship he had never had. Perhaps the therapist's too-strict adherence to the "rules" of analytically oriented psychotherapy for this obsessional patient felt like sadistic withholding.

The therapist's interpretations in fact were "penetrating". The total situation's being experienced as both stimulating and frustrating could be seen as attributable to the reality of how the patient and therapist were in fact behaving together, as conceivably could be evident to an outside observer. Thus, the patient's experiencing the therapy as an enema, supposedly cleansing and healing, but also intrusive, overstimulating, and overpowering, could be attributed as much to the factual reality of what therapist and patient were doing in the present, as it could to the reawakening of past memories/fantasies/impulses/ defenses relating to the father in the past. The "purely" neutral stance of the therapist may have had real impact in the present and may have caused iatrogenic effects, making it impossible to discern what was being stimulated in the "now", and what was being "transferred".

We might wonder, had the therapist been willing and able to be somewhat more flexible, would the outcome have been different? For example, the therapist might have been a bit more gratifying of the patient's pleas for acknowledgement that he had a point, that he was at least somewhat correct in how he was interpreting his own experience. The therapist's omission of any of his countertransference feelings in his report may be indicative of his not noticing or considering them as essential data during the therapy, so that he may have deprived himself of internal indicators suggesting that he was in fact really treating the patient as the patient remembered/fantasized his father had treated him. The patient remembered being carried home from school when sick in his father's arms. Perhaps if the therapist had recognized that this was how the patient was experiencing, or wished/feared to experience the therapy, he might have been able to discuss such wishes/fears in a way that not only would have let the patient feel understood, but also to some degree gratified and reassured. That is, had the therapist been more giving, more natural in his interactions, more like a real person, more self-disclosing, the transference situation might have become less intensely frightening.

Had the therapist more obviously participated personally, the patient might have experienced a greater sense of collaborative mutuality, so that he might have been able to tolerate staying and pursuing the work further. The therapist seemed to rely upon interpretation alone to extricate the patient from the overwhelming repetition of his relationship with his father in the transference. One could argue that a greater chance of success might have been provided by both providing and acknowledging with the patient a new experience that was real.

A classical therapist might reply that this patient would have brought his pre-existing maladaptive solutions to his conflicts to the therapy, regardless of the therapist he was seeing. If the therapist had consciously adjusted his behavior so as to escape the transference role thrust upon him, thus providing a "corrective experience", he would in effect have been interfering with the blossoming of the transference. That is, the patient's potential to realize the extent to which his negative view of his father may have been a fantastical creation of his own unconscious might have been compromised by taking it too literally as something that needed to be "corrected". To gratify the patient with self-revelation, real participation, or reassurance would have avoided the tensions inherent in the patient's own latently present, multiple, conflictual perspectives. Presenting himself in reality, the therapist would dilute transference potentiality, which ideally could be discoverable to the patient's benefit. Presenting himself as a "good object", he would have mollified the potential development of the negative transference.

This patient escaped full transference development by terminating the treatment prematurely. The question remains as to whether he would have been better helped had he been persuaded to remain in treatment by whatever means, e.g., by the therapist becoming more forcefully convincing, or whether he was in fact best served by experiencing as much of his negative transference as he could tolerate. In the final analysis it is not possible to know how the treatment would have unfolded differently had the therapist used a different approach. Nor is it possible to know which of the alternative methods, whether based upon the "old" or the "new" view of transference, would have resulted in the greatest clinical benefit for the patient in the long run. Carefully designed, prospective research studies might one day provide some answers.

Chapter Twelve

Short Vignettes of Dynamically Oriented Psychotherapy

This chapter presents a number of shorter vignettes (many previously published) (Goldstein 1996) of dynamically oriented psychotherapy. Although not detailed like previous chapters, these vignettes provide an overview of this form of psychotherapy. They demonstrate therapy that uses a strong therapeutic alliance to explore dynamic situations in the present (outside of the transference) and to help understand these current situations by correlations with the past.

VIGNETTE 1: AN INSIGHT-ORIENTED APPROACH WITH AN ACTING-OUT PATIENT

Dr. L, a middle-aged, moderately successful physician, was incredibly sensitive to being treated unfairly, with a tendency toward rapid rage on these occasions and ensuing acting out. All this happened almost at a stimulus-response level. For example, a truck driver cut off Dr. L and within seconds he challenged the driver to a fight. On another occasion a colleague treated Dr. L discourteously on the phone, to which Dr. L uttered a few choice words and hung up. Work in the therapy sessions focused on attempts to slow down these stimulus-response type reactions. As one example after another came up, Dr. L gradually was able to experience and tolerate painful feeling states that corresponded to his being treated so unfairly. As he began to replace his usual acting with thinking, he was able to link these uncomfortable shameful feelings to previously unconscious self-representations of being inadequate and passive. Genetic exploration traced this to repetitive experiences of being embarrassed and even humiliated by his father. With years of focusing on the sequence of frustration, uncomfortable feeling state, painful self-representation, and defensive acting out, Dr. L was able to alter his usual impulsive behavior. Psychotherapy with Dr. L took place somewhat in accordance with the model of defensive change via insight. In this example, understanding occurred without direct reliving of the experiences in the transference.

VIGNETTE 2: INSIGHT ORIENTED THERAPY WITH A PATIENT WHO CRAVED STIMULATION

Mr. V was a young lawyer to whom stimulation became a way of life. Although functioning in a superior manner professionally, nights and weekends were filled with excitement and stimulation. After work, Mr. V would head to the bars and to the dance halls, where he sought exotic and attractive women. These women, typically unstable and needy, formed clinging and dependent relationships with Mr. V rather rapidly. Weekends were spent at other forms of recreation: mountain climbing, hiking, boating, and caving. Vacations were used to go on cross-country bike trips or abroad to the most exotic countries. Mr. V viewed these activities without anxiety and as commonplace.

Occasional breaks from these nonstop activities led to feelings akin to emptiness or nothingness. Mr. V came to appreciate that ordinary activities did not help rid himself of these uncomfortable feelings; nor did the usual professional women with whom he regularly associated. He needed stimulation and activity well beyond the ordinary. The therapist was able to help Mr. V to understand that the stimulating activities and exotic women were ways of dealing with these very uncomfortable feelings.

Mr. V described a childhood devoid of fun and amusement, where everything was totally serious. With this atmosphere, related to tragedies that both of his parents had suffered, Mr. V early on sought out both soothing and excitement. As Mr. V was able to identify his feelings of emptiness and nothingness, to relate these feelings to his childhood environment, and to understand his tendency toward stimulating and exciting activities and people as a defense against those feelings, he was gradually able to turn to events and people at least somewhat more ordinary. By the end of therapy, Mr. V had married an ordinary professional woman and had replaced the stimulating activities by more exciting aspects of his profession.

The model of therapy with Mr. V was in accordance with change via interpretation of dysphoric affect and defense. Understanding again occurred with only minimal overt focus on the transference.

VIGNETTE 3: FOCUS ON THE WORKING ALLIANCE WITH A PATIENT WITH A RELENTLESS SUPEREGO

Mr. H, a high powered achievement-oriented professional, continually set up exalted, idealistic, and often very unrealistic aspirations and goals. He felt obligated to fulfill these goals at all times without exception. When he failed to meet his expectations, he criticized himself in the most harsh and relentless way. He would verbally berate himself, at times for hours. These verbal beatings took the form of accusing himself of being undeserving, inadequate, a piece of trash. He shouldn't have been born; he deserved to die! Beatings took place for a variety of events, ranging from not achieving more at work, not being a better son or friend, or seemingly insignificant items like not cleaning his room or failing to exercise. At times Mr. H beat himself for having physical difficulties, such as headaches or the flu.

In the course of therapy, Mr. H was able to arrive at a fair amount of insight. He understood the idealism and the grandiosity behind his unreasonable goals. He understood the extreme harshness and viciousness of his superego attacks. He understood the gratification involved in these attacks, and how they could be sexualized at times. He understood that the beatings stopped him from moving forward in work and with relationships. He understood the triggers and precipitants to the symptoms. He had a decent understanding of the genetic correlates to the problem, including specific early memories involving his parents and brothers. Although ameliorated somewhat in frequency and intensity, the beatings continued.

At this point therapeutic focus changed to an examination of how, despite his understanding, the symptoms recurred. There was a direct focus on the observing ego. What stopped Mr. H from using his observing ego to take a look at what was happening, gain perspective, and take action to stop his symptoms? Exploration revealed that the failure to involve the observing ego was itself a passive defense against being assertive. The above type of exploration allowed Mr. H to eventually gain more control over his symptoms.

With Mr. H, the therapy, including the focus on the observing ego, remained at an exploratory level. Yet there was little evidence of the dynamics described occurring within the transference. Thus the treatment was clearly that of a dynamically oriented psychotherapy.

VIGNETTE 4: WORK WITH A VERY SUICIDAL AND SOMETIMES PSYCHOTIC PATIENT

A teenage patient with intermittent suicidal ideation had been in psychotherapy for a number of years. Initially she concealed her suicidal ideation. On several occasions she came close to acting, but fortunately her plans were discovered by the therapist in time for preventative hospitalizations. As might be evident at this point, the establishment of a therapeutic alliance was quite difficult, with several brief terminations in the early years. Later, when the alliance became stronger, the patient was able to share her symptom of intermittent auditory hallucinations with the therapist.

With the sharing of the voices, patient and therapist were able to establish a sequence that the voices followed, that allowed for early hospitalization at times of clear suicidal threat, before there was legitimate risk of acting. The voices started as sounds, then progressed to inaudible words, then to words that the patient could hear but which had no understandable meaning. The words then took on meaning, but the meaning was vague. Then there were vague suicide ideas, followed by clear suicide ideas, followed by commands. In the command stage the patient at first did not listen to them, then was worried that she might. Of interest was the fact that the patient never thought the voices were of other people; she always maintained reality testing in that she viewed the voices as her own.

As the patient was able to reveal the above sequence, it became rather obvious at what point hospitalization as needed. With the establishment of the sequence, patient and therapist felt comfortable working on the dynamics of the voices without fear of acting out. As the dynamics were elucidated in the therapy sessions, the sequence would stop, usually with the voices decreasing in the same order in which they had originally occurred. Precipitants to the voices were learned about first, then the vulnerabilities underlying the precipitants. As understanding increased, the voices decreased, so that by the termination of therapy, they had virtually ended.

In this vignette the severe acting out could only be contained after a suitable therapeutic alliance was established. At this point therapist and patient were able to work collaboratively to use the sequence of voices as signals to impending acting out. As the voices came closer to signaling action, either dynamic understanding was successful enough to send the voices in the opposite direction, or hospitalization was mutually agreed upon. Before the emergence of a reasonable therapeutic alliance, only hospitalization could prevent action. In this vignette, the possibility of hospitalization plus the establishment of a reasonable therapeutic alliance combined to make dynamically oriented therapy workable. There was little overt focus on the transference after the therapeutic alliance became strengthened.

VIGNETTE 5: INSIGHT ORIENTED WORK WITH A PATIENT WHO ACTS OUT WITH ANXIETIES REGARDING SUCCESS

Mr. J, a young accountant, was involved in several incidents of unfortunate acting out in efforts to ward off acute anxiety and fears of catastrophe. He had left his previous job abruptly, after his anxiety rose to an intolerable level. He had then wandered around the country for several months, gradually calming down. Recently he had taken a job similar to the first one. Sensing his anxiety level again beginning to rise, he entered psychotherapy.

On the surface things had gone well in his previous job. Mr. J was well liked, did good work, always acted agreeably, and had been promoted rather rapidly. Yet he had become increasingly anxious and uncomfortable. He was particularly bothered by the lack of an overtly positive attitude by his boss and by a perceived lack of appreciation by his colleagues. He wanted his boss to give him regular feedback, make sure he had the best working conditions, offer advice, give praise when appropriate, and, in general, to act in a fatherly manner. He wanted his colleagues to overtly appreciate his skills, to offer encouragement, and to reach out to him socially.

It was not that his boss and colleagues were not positive to him; in fact they were. However, both disappointed him in accordance with his idealistic and unrealistic expectations. As his expectations remained unfulfilled and he became increasingly disappointed and discontent with the various perceived deficiencies of his workplace, Mr. J began to experience a lack of energy, enthusiasm, and well-being. He began to brood, then became overtly angry. Work felt more and more negative to him, and he began to dislike being there. As his anger increased, he became anxious that he might have a major confrontation, with fantasies of getting fired, or of fist fights. When the anger and anxiety reached an intolerable level, he abruptly quit.

As far as his social life was concerned, Mr. J had been dating a young woman for several years. The relationship was reasonable, mutual, and intimate. When the idea of marriage came up, however, he began to feel panicky. He was worried about all sorts of issues, from the type of wedding ceremony to the raising of the children. He began to feel coerced and forced to marry against his will, with fantasies of being made passive and weak. Ultimately he feared that marriage would be a catastrophe, limiting his freedom and individuality. As his anxiety increased, he abruptly ended the relationship.

Mr. J began therapy in a very tenuous and ambivalent way, missing a number of sessions, typically being late, and continually talking about quitting. After this shaky start, he settled down and gradually formed a mildly idealized transference, out of which a reasonable therapeutic alliance developed. Within that setting he began to focus on difficulties and conflicts with his new job and with a new girlfriend. The conflicts that were instrumental in ending his previous work situation and relationship reoccurred. This time Mr. J was able to explore them, in a supportive environment, so that he did not act out. By a process of continual clarification of his conflicts and with intermittent definite suggestion (not to abandon under frustration either the job or the girlfriend), he was able to move ahead in both areas. With time the suggestion (not to act under frustration) was no longer needed.

Regarding the work situation, Mr. J learned that his expectations were far too idealistic and far too unrealistic. Although reasonable on the surface, what he wanted and expected just did not happen in the real world. Although the ideal boss might call his employees in for frequent evaluations, give them encouragement and praise, and make sure their working conditions were optimal, bosses rarely act like that. Although ideally coworkers might treat one with sensitivity, appreciation, and respect, the usual milieu in Mr. J's (and any other) workplace was more likely to expose one to sarcastic comments and competition. As he began to realize that his expectations were related to his underlying desire and need to have a totally concerned, supportive, appreciative and empathic father, Mr. J was able to lower these expectations and become more accepting at work. As noted, the therapist was perceived as a concerned, supportive, appreciative and empathic father, although he never acted any differently than a reasonably skilled, dedicated, and concerned therapist.

Regarding his relationship with his girlfriend, as the possibility of permanency came up, Mr. J again became increasingly anxious. He felt that marriage would close off opportunities, and he fantasized numerous catastrophes. Again he entertained fantasies of being coerced and made passive by his girlfriend. Actually the girlfriend was quite giving and flexible, most frequently capitulating to Mr. J's wishes. Conflicts about feeling forced, coerced, and made passive (in relationship to the girlfriend) were brought into the therapy and examined. Mr. J's marked vulnerability in this area was noted, together with the reality of his dominance vis-à-vis his girlfriend. Alternative possibilities to his fantasized catastrophes of the marriage were presented. The fact that he had run from several other relationships was explored. Reasons for ending the current relationship were noted to be related to his conflicts rather than the girlfriend's characteristics. At one point it was noted that this particular girlfriend might have traits that actually complemented his conflicts. Thus, with repetitive clarification, offering alternative perspectives of reality, and with overt suggestion (not to run), Mr. J was able to pursue the relationship, ultimately deciding on marriage. In the six months preceding the marriage, the therapist refrained from additional suggestions. Regarding the discussion of the relationship, Mr. J felt supported by the therapist, who was again seen as a mildly idealized father figure, interested in his needs, showing respect for his conflicts, and appreciating his points of view.

Work with Mr. J included a genetic component focusing on the father. Viewed as unsupportive, unempathic, and lacking in many ways, the father had the habit of exposing his son to the most anxiety-provoking situations. The son would feel coerced to participate in activities against his will, resulting in states of acute anxiety. Still, the father was admired and idealized, and Mr. J was clearly disappointed and devastated by his early death. Genetic material regarding the father was related in the therapy hours to Mr. J's ideals and expectations with peers and supervisors, to his tendency to feel coerced, forced, and made passive, and to his proclivity for episodes of acute anxiety and fears of catastrophe.

The psychotherapy with Mr. J began by focusing on a very tenuous therapeutic alliance. After many interventions aimed at strengthening the alliance, related to numerous disruptions in the therapy, a mildly idealized transference evolved, along with a good therapeutic alliance. The idealized transference was helpful in the maintenance of the therapeutic alliance and was left largely uninterpreted. Interventions were mainly insight oriented. However, to block destructive acting out, both suggestion and reality clarification in the form of offering alternate perspectives were utilized. As with the last vignette, there was little overt focus on the transference once the therapeutic alliance was clearly established.

VIGNETTE 6: A VERY SUPPORTIVE APPROACH WITH A PARANOID PATIENT

This last vignette uses an approach clearly more supportive than the others in this chapter. Here supportive interventions played a larger role than insight oriented ones. Supportive techniques included the strengthening of selected adaptive defenses, suggestion, education, limit setting, reality testing, and encouragement. In this vignette a strong therapeutic alliance is the essential psychotherapeutic tool. With the alliance in place, difficult current dynamics could be explored. Compared to other cases in this chapter there was less focus on the past. This vignette demonstrates a very supportive approach, tangential to that of the more usually dynamically oriented psychotherapies in this chapter.

Mr. C was a 34-year-old married man, the father of three children, successfully employed for a number of years as a truck driver. He came for psychotherapy with the chief complaint that innuendoes were going around suggesting that he was homosexual. These innuendoes were conveyed to him by various subtleties, such as someone's putting his finger on his eyebrow, starting at Mr. C's groin area, or motioning to Mr. C in a certain manner. On several occasions, Mr. C became quite upset by the intimations and got into fist fights. The innuendoes had been bothering Mr. C for three months, during which time he also had recurrent obsessive thoughts that others thought he was homosexual. Except during the episodes of fighting, Mr. C kept his ideas of the allusions to himself. He had no idea why people would want to convey these suggestions to him.

Mr. C was a large, muscular man, very athletic, a weight lifter for years. He got along well with his co-workers but suffered from recurrent thoughts that others might not like him. He devoted a lot of time to his family and was fond of both his wife and children. Sexual relations with his wife were sporadic and characterized by occasional impotency and premature ejaculation. When Mr. C did not perform up to his expectations sexually, he became anxious and depressed. Mr. C had a history, in the last five years, of secret heterosexual affairs, in which he performed quite adequately. Mr. C had no history of either homosexuality or of paranoid ideation until the present episode.

With Mr. C the establishment of a strong therapeutic alliance came easily. With this alliance in place, support was given to Mr. C to assure him that, indeed, he was not homosexual, as evidenced by his muscular appearance, his proclivity for sports, his string of affairs with women, and the fact that he had never had an overt homosexual experience. Thus, the reaction formations used by the patient in everyday life to prove to himself that he was not homosexual were supported and were used as evidence to reinforce for Mr. C that, despite the innuendoes, he, indeed, was not homosexual.

The following contradiction was pointed out to Mr. C. On the one hand, he clearly was not homosexual; yet, on the other, he was constantly being disturbed by homosexual innuendoes. He even suffered from recurring thoughts questioning his sexuality. Could it be that, for some reason, he was sensitive and vulnerable to the idea that he might be homosexual? Mr. C latched onto this concept willingly and happily. It was like a revelation to him. With this insight, limit setting was initiated easily. Mr. C was encouraged not to act on the homosexual innuendoes. Reminding him again of his vulnerability in this area, he was asked if it might not be useful to delay action and to talk in psychotherapy instead. Would it not be more helpful to consider all the different possibilities about why, for example, someone rubbed his eyebrow, to ponder about this action at length, to ruminate over it, rather than to immediately conclude that it was a homosexual innuendo? At all costs Mr. C should delay acting until he had a chance to talk in his therapy hours.

In the therapy sessions Mr. C was asked if his sensitivity in this area might not lead him to relate other people's actions to his own area of conflict. Being sensitive, might he not tend to personalize? When faced with an area of ambiguity, might he not think too rapidly in terms of homosexual innuendoes? What other possibilities were there? With each occurrence of what Mr. C perceived as a homosexual innuendo, he brought into the psychotherapy a detailed account of what actually transpired. With a repetitive examination of the details, it was easy to focus on the area of ambiguity and to help show Mr. C how he so often prematurely latched onto explanations involving homosexual innuendoes. With repetitive reality testing, Mr. C became increasingly able to see his distortions and to make adaptations in this area.

The final step in the psychotherapy with Mr. C was to help him understand what external events and life stresses made him particularly prone to think in terms of homosexual innuendoes. Mr. C focused on three areas that caused him difficulty: inadequate performance with his wife, being the subject of jokes about his muscular physique, and rejections in his pursuit of extramarital affairs. Mr. C learned, whenever he exposed himself to one of these three major areas of danger, to immediately think about his sensitivity and to be on guard against ensuing distortions.

Chapter Thirteen

Fully Developed Transference and Its Resolution in Psychoanalysis

PREFACING REMARKS

While our previous illustrations presented either fragments of a course of psychotherapy, or a treatment process interrupted prematurely, we here present a full nine-year psychoanalysis of a middle-aged professional woman, as described by the analyst, retrospectively. We include this lengthy case report to demonstrate the full, natural unfolding of a florid transference neurosis and its resolution, in which all aspects of character (drives, defenses, moral concerns, past object relations) are engaged, enveloping the relationship with the therapist. This case report also shows the working through of acting out and enactment as resistances, and the increasing intensification of the therapy, by which the patient could let herself experience so-called primitive affects, dreams, fantasies, and urges. These could then be recruited by the creative, progressive, synthetic aspects of her mind, and integrated via self-reflection, leading through a fully experienced and explored termination phase to a successful outcome with real personality change.

The male therapist largely maintained, in his therapeutic behavior and interventions, a technically neutral, abstinent, classical stance. His technique derived from an ego-psychological model, by which he emphasized addressing defenses which the patient employed against drive derivatives. However, as he describes, he was consciously aware of the intersubjective aspects of his relationship with the patient, and acknowledged to himself that his own inner experience, perceptions, and thoughts about the patient and about the course of the analysis probably were affected by unconscious aspects of his relationship with her. Perhaps, in ways he could not notice, his demeanor and technique were also countertransferentially affected. The patient was quite responsive to the analytic approach and able to delve deeply into the transference.

While, for clarity's sake, we have sharply distinguished the "old" and "new" views of transference, in fact they include each other. While the "old" view emphasizes transference of aspects of relationships from the past, it acknowledges that it is essential to take into account the present interactions with the real person of the therapist. Conversely, the significance of past relationships is not ignored by the "new" view, which emphasizes the transference as occurring in the real situation that is present.

According to the "new" view, transference may be merely one side of a newly created, thoroughly dyadic real relationship. The patient is affected by the immediate actuality of the person of the therapist as he objectively presents himself. The patient also is affected by the therapist's subjective inner experience, even if the therapist thinks he keeps it private. Communicated to the patient are aspects of the outward behavior and inner experience of the therapist that are both conscious and unconscious. The inward, implicit aspect may be conveyed nonverbally, the patient perceiving it perhaps subliminally.

Likewise, the patient reciprocally communicates nonverbally and subliminally, affecting the therapist. As Freud (1912a) said, the unconscious of one person, remarkably, can be in communication with the unconscious of another. This reciprocal, mutual dimension of perhaps affectively powerful, meaningful yet unconscious, nonverbal communication may issue in "enactments," as will be seen in this case. Yet, as important as is this inter-subjective/relational experience in the continuous dynamic interaction, i.e., the presently created real relationship between the two people, it would be a mistake to forget that each person also brings along his or her past.

Past experiences of important persons, circumstances, and events have impressed themselves upon everyone's mental apparatus and character. Incorporated as memories, tendencies, and fantasies into the pre-existing mental "structures" which form new experiences, those past experiences now "color" the glasses through which the person views and responds to present-day events and relationships. Thus, transference is not merely the patient's experience of the therapist in the present, but must include experience of the past speaking through the present.

The relationship between past and present, however, is a two-way street. Present experience in the transference also impresses itself back upon the mental apparatus, engaging and impinging upon the fantasy/memory structures which were the precipitates of past relationships and events, thus also activating impulse, affect, cognition, and defense. Stimulated by the present reality with the therapist, the mind actively works things over in relation to the memories or representations of persons from the past not actually present, thus arriving at new reconciliations or compromises. Thus, the structures (derived from past experience) which form new experience are also altered by that new experience. Psychoanalysis thus can change a person lastingly and profoundly.

INITIAL PRESENTATION AND HISTORY OF THE PATIENT

This school administrator was 39-years-old when she was referred for psychoanalysis after many years of previous therapy, with the chief complaint being, "I don't have any real feelings. I've distanced myself from almost all relationships. They seem empty to me. I don't want to become rigid and closed-off for good." Though she had close friends, she perceived that she had become aloof, indifferent, even callous toward others. She felt she had to maintain a facade of toughness, saying, "It's as if I wrote a part for myself in a script, and I can't stop; I'm locked into it."

She had become depressed following her divorce two years earlier, ending her two-year marriage. "I really had taken it as 'till death do us part.' When we broke up, it was like finding out there is no Santa Claus. I felt it was my fault." After the divorce, she had a few relationships and then had largely stopped dating. She feared there would be no one else for her to depend upon, that she might become destitute.

The patient, for her first 12 years, lived in an impoverished rural Midwestern small town. She was the next to youngest of three daughters and a brother in a blue-collar fundamentalist family. They lived among rats and roaches. The only toilet was at the foot of her parents' bed. She remembers early on feeling resentment at her parents for being inadequate providers, who were unable to protect her. She felt intimidated by her father, who, constantly simmering with rage, rarely spoke to her. "I wasn't sure if he even knew my name." Realizing as a teenager at her very first job that she was earning more than her father, she was mortified. Mother could be cold and angry, saying, "You want to cry? I'll give you something to cry about!" The patient was sexually molested at age 11 by a trusted adult male neighbor. She became ashamed of her background, and vowed to herself that she would improve her condition in life. As she in fact did advance in stature professionally and socially, she came to feel "an imposter," however, who could be found out.

Opening Phase of Treatment: Early Sexualization of the Transference and Resistance Activated

In the first evaluation session, the patient opened with the tongue-in-cheek statement: "I know that what's supposed to happen here is that I fall in love with you, you fall in love with me, and we get married." It soon became obvious that she was above average in intelligence, quite verbal and imaginative, with an engaging sense of humor, even as she told of her difficult history. In the first several weeks of the analysis there occurred a rapid intensification and sexualization of the transference, which I may have inadvertently promoted by a countertransferential attitude, that she was needful and that I should give her ideas, interactions, and reassurance. She expressed wishes, without expecting their fulfillment that I would hold her hand, or come lie beside her on the couch. She chided me for seeming to be nice and awakening in her wishes to be close to somebody, but felt the dilemma: "How can I get involved, if I know that everything will have to end eventually?"

Defensive maneuvers seemed aimed at preventing these wishes for involvement with me from becoming too strong or too elaborated consciously. Thus, she would intellectualize and consciously censor her thoughts. She attempted to deaden her feelings, getting sleepy in the sessions, or to discount their significance by making editorial comments, such as, "My feelings are so infantile!" When she did allow herself to express sadness or longing, she would get angry with herself and have the thought, "Oh, big fucking deal! Grow up already!" I might point out at such a moment that she was treating herself as she might have expected her mother to treat her. In general, though, most of my comments were aimed at demonstrating to her her defensive maneuver at the moment, and wondering with her why it seemed necessary just then. I might offer a conjecture about her motivations for the defense, based on the immediately manifest content. That is, I tried to clarify her conflict at the surface at the moment. For example, a typical comment from me would be, "I wonder if getting sleepy right now helps you get away from those wishes for closeness that seem so unacceptable to you." Likewise, I would point out if she would use humor to minimize the importance of what she had reported.

By the ninth month, she felt the analysis had become a "trap" for her. For example, she remembered a high school teacher who over several years pursued a special, supportive relationship with her, showing kindness and generosity: "You can love him and be excited in that passive sort of way, because it's safe and you know nothing will happen." Eventually, however, he made physical advances. She recoiled in horror. It seemed to me that she was allowing herself to feel such closeness in the treatment, transferring the memories of the "safe" relationship, along with the ambivalence and anticipated betrayal of trust, into the relationship with me. She felt "at a disadvantage. The more I tell you, the worse things are." Feeling "not safe here," she remembered being tricked into a date with a coworker when she was young and innocent: "But then I got angry with myself. Maybe I'd only played innocent. Maybe I'd set myself up."

Comment:

From the new perspective, the transference feelings were activated because the analyst and the patient actually were together, affecting one another in the present. She appeared needful; he felt the urge to help. She responded with wishes for more intimacy. Their interactions in fact were real. Even from that point of view, we can see the feelings, urges, and fears activated in the patient also evoked memories (the teacher, the co-worker—both men who in some way took advantage of her) that involved the very same feelings, urges, and fears, uncannily. One could theorize that those specific memories were the ones activated because the ambience between the patient and therapist at that moment was very specifically evocative. On the other hand, from the old perspective, one would theorize that the transference unfolded in this particular way because the unconscious past within the patient, represented in memories of those experiences of seduction, which were associated with latent feelings and drives, would be in effect vigilant, seeking and waiting for an opportunity in the present by which to express themselves. The past would be shaping the present. Thus again, the new and old theoretical perspectives are not mutually exclusive, but integrate with each other.

Hearing these memories, I pointed out how she feared her wishes for closeness would lead her to repeat a situation in which she would be abused, and maybe she would feel responsible. "Perhaps these fears are operating here," I said. The next day, she reported a dream in which a car pulled up and six people wanted to come into her house. She was scared and tried to keep them out. Then, she was in the car. "The guy driving it was the scariest kind of hillbilly [this would be a characterization she might give of her family]. He had four gold teeth. I was sitting on his lap. And on the car seat was the biggest dollar bill I'd ever seen—I took the bill and tried to run away—I was wearing these really tight hot pants. He made some comment about my tattoo. He might have been referring to this tiny birthmark I have, here," (and to show where, she patted herself on the side of her buttock).

I thought she in the dream was fearing her urges to "break into my house," seduce me, and steal my "big dollar." I said to her, "You might be frightened that if you let yourself be fully involved in the analysis, and believe you can get from me what you really need, you might feel like you're going along with something 'sleazy' [her word], unacceptable, and scary." When in the next week, I appeared to have a cold and coughed, she said, "You should be home in bed, and I should come over there." After hesitation, which I inquired about, she added, "My next thought was that I should be in bed with you. But then, I wouldn't want to leave." She tried to reverse these thoughts. I pointed out her fear that saying them might lead to their coming true. She was excited by the possibility of seducing me, but also frightened by it.

Comment:

We might surmise that the therapist's interpretation of her fears that her wishes for closeness would lead her into an abusive situation, and his connecting that state of mind to her feelings in the therapy situation, may have contributed to instigating, or permitting the emergence of, the dream. Notice her allusions in the dream to her family ("hillbillies") and to the theme of seductiveness. The therapist thought this revealed some key conflictual issues which, "transferred" into the treatment, frightened her. His interpreting this showed his understanding of her dilemma in an empathic manner. The increased sense of safety that resulted probably contributed to the emergence of yet further such "material" (the fantasies of being in bed with the therapist), paradoxically raising again her anxieties.

The therapist thought she was fearing her active wishes to "break into [the therapist's] house and seduce [him]" and so forth. One might wonder, couldn't she have been fearing the opposite, that the therapist was the frightening hillbilly seducer, and she still the frightened victim? In fact, both of these seemingly opposite interpretations might have been valid. We might think of the "scary" aggressive seducer as one side of a dyadic internal object relation, paired with the frightened overwhelmed victim. One pole of the pair might at a given time represent her "self", the other pole, her "object" representation. At another time, the roles of "self" and "object" may be reversed. Such a reversal in fact occurred during the course of the very same dream, in which she switched from being frightened, trying to keep the intruder out, to sitting in hot pants on his lap. Her patting herself in the session implied an active urge to recreate the scenario in the therapy with the therapist. He nevertheless evidently at that time thought that to speak to her as frightened was more consistent with and acceptable to the self-image that at that time was conscious.

Thus, by the end of the first year, the transference had become sexually quite charged. A very attractive woman, she once came to the session in a low-cut T-shirt with obviously no bra. Once, she had her leg flexed, so that her dress fell toward her lap, nearly fully revealing her thigh. I was not immune to these seductive charms, though, needless to say, I don't believe I ever fell from an appropriate professional or therapeutic stance. Nevertheless, the erotic haze may have obscured at times my clear awareness of the unconscious aggression she was also expressing, in effect, "assaulting my defenses" (like the hillbillies at the door). At the time, I did not feel that I could explicitly address this body language, fearing that to do so would be too hurtful narcissistically for the patient. I thought that she was expressing urges from multiple developmental levels simultaneously—on the one hand, to win me as a good mother and be cared for; on the other hand, to seduce and thus injure me. I thought she was trying to repeat with me past traumata of overstimulation, turning passive into active, seducing the powerful man, getting revenge on "the dirty neighbor". Still, I decided to confine myself to addressing what was manifest or preconscious in her verbal material, on the assumption that deeper material would eventually emerge and psychological change would occur through uncovering and interpreting at the surface, i.e., what she could acknowledge in the medium of speech. My key motto, for better or worse, seems to have been, "Patience".

Comment:

This analyst acknowledges in his report to us that he was affected by the patient's erotic transference behaviors. He willfully confined himself to "proper neutral and professional technique", but we might wonder if his inner, silent responses nevertheless may have been subliminally communicated to the patient, "despite himself". Many would argue that her effects on him in any case inevitably would become a substantial component of their transference-countertransference "unified structure", their shared fantasy, conscious and unconscious, even if unacknowledged from the therapist's side.

At about this time, she began again a practice from her adolescence and early twenties, shoplifting. She felt "compelled to". I wondered if she put it that way in order not to notice her motivations. I pointed out how she in effect was saying to me, "If you won't take care of me, I'll take care of myself." She felt she had never had enough. The shoplifting also seemed to compensate for a perception of herself as somehow defective. This sense of defect appeared frequently in her thoughts about her body. It also presented itself in her thoughts about her position relative to men: Who needs whom more? Who is more capable? Feeling disadvantaged in having been born female, she undertook weightlifting to be able to outperform men in physical strength. She thought of a powerful boyfriend and said, "I wanted to *be* him." I pointed out, "Being like an indestructible man would remove you from feelings of weakness and vulnerability you feel a woman has." She said, "Right. I make it up sexually. They have to beg *me* to give them something." She then introduced a jargon-term jokingly, saying she had "terminal penis envy." "Whenever men are around, I feel and act stupid and incompetent. . . . I had to be that way with my father, because he was stupid and I didn't want to seem more competent than him. God, I hate him. He was a real prick." She went on to describe wanting a man as a good-looking trinket, who needn't say much: "I should buy one." She then laughed uproariously as she realized, "That's what I'm doing with you. But I don't want to think about you; then I'll want too much, even to be inside you. Maybe that's my problem with sex: *I* want to get inside."

She had a dream in which I was leading her across a snowy mountain; we were walking side by side. "But I was walking close to this edge that was very steep, and when I looked, it seemed very dangerous. The path was icy. I felt a little scared. . . . Why should I be thinking of *you* in my bed?!" She went on to sexual thoughts and wondered, "What if you felt the same way about me? That would be really scary." I commented, "As if you'd pull me down the slippery slope with you." She replied, "Right. That would be fun." I said, "Fun, but scary." It was becoming explicit, as she spoke of her hatred of and wishing to kill all men, that her sexual wishes toward me involved not only erotic but also destructive impulses.

Comment:

We can perhaps see the value here of the analyst's not having told the patient of his countertransference reactions. His abstinence gave her the "psychological space" to expand her awareness and expression of her fantasies and feelings without fear of consequences becoming too real. Nevertheless, we might wonder whether his comment, "Fun, but scary," may have been inadvertently seductive on the therapist's part, as if he were agreeing that he would also find it fun to be pulled down the slippery slope with her. Once again, we can see how subtle can be the process by which a therapist may begin to enact countertransferentially with a patient, without being at all aware of doing so.

Enactment

Largely unconsciously, these wishes were expressed at the beginning of the third year, in her handling of the fee and financial arrangements with me. In the third year, she didn't send the bills in to the insurance company, kept vague about her finances, and fell several thousand dollars in debt to me. On the one hand, this debt supported consciously her view of herself as helpless and needing me as a benefactor. On the other hand, this apparent helplessness disguised her powerful assertion of control, as if to say, "Somebody has to pay for what happened to me." I thought she was trying unconsciously to take advantage, to "shoplift" from me. She was seizing control, but felt helpless in doing so. She had said that money and sex felt the same to her. I pointed out that to give me money too freely might feel like giving me sex. To pay would feel like cooperating in being abused. She felt like a little girl who was being asked to do too much, to do something grown up. Withholding the money felt like turning the tables on me, but she feared she would get me angry with her. On the one hand, she imagined our fighting over the payment would create an emotional distance she would find reassuring, but on the other hand, she feared I might "strangle" her. Withholding the money thus involved stimulating fantasies of provoking me to abuse her. She felt repeatedly "screwed over" in life, abused, unprotected, and corrupted. I pointed out how to pay me would feel like joining me in doing something wrong and dirty.

She wanted to provoke me to act emotionally with her, both to win and to lose me. At three and one-half years, she reported a dream taking place near my office, in which she haughtily taunted a man who had dropped his stick. She then feared his reaction, as if she would be sexually molested. I said, "By not paying the fee, you may be pointing out how I've dropped my stick." She responded, "It's true. It shows you're powerless to make me pay. It's like I'm kicking somebody while he's down and saying, 'Get up and fight!' I'm such a sadist, a sick person. I need to find fault, to keep from feeling too dependent. I always have one foot out the door with relationships, to decrease my vulnerability to being left. I allow feelings about you to creep in a little bit, but there's a longing to be cared for, like I were little. Of course, you could kick me out of the treatment." I pointed out, "One of the meanings of the deficit with the fee could be that it's a way to keep a distance from me over which you can have control."

She was able to see the dream as obviously referring to her relationship with me, and was now able to see that not paying was acting-out, with multiple meanings. Yet, she was still doing it. I noted that she thought of my kicking her out of the treatment as a defense against the thought of staying and enjoying her sadistic power over me. She couldn't permit herself at that point to experience loving closeness with me, for fear that she would injure or destroy me, or provoke me to get rid of her, and then she would have nothing. I pointed out that to not pay me helped her feel that she didn't have the right to demand too much from me. She feared depleting me, as indicated by thoughts of "kittens eating up their mother." Her solution to these dilemmas was to stay stuck in a morass of passive-aggressive sadomasochistic acting-out, from which at this point she only intermittently could extricate herself enough to see clearly what she was doing.

From my present perspective, while I was consciously and explicitly trying to analyze her withholding payments, the fact that I continued to see her and tolerate that reality may have constituted an enactment that consolidated her resistance and reinforced her staying stuck. We were avoiding the enraged feelings that she may have expressed were I to have frustrated her and demanded payment; perhaps I had let myself be seduced unknowingly. That is, my interest in continuing to see her, fully justified by therapeutic intent and objective clinical assessment, nevertheless may also have derived from more subjective, less conscious responses to her manner of presenting herself to me and her treatment of me. She was working hard to try to make me reject her, and I, without quite realizing it, was working hard to reassure her that I would not. My countertransference wish (which happened to coincide with my professional judgment of what was best) was to keep her in treatment. Nevertheless, in trying to be tolerant, neutral and understanding, I accepted mistreatment. One again might wonder if perhaps it would have been better to have taken a more confrontational stance. I might have said something like, "You're noticing that despite your efforts, things aren't changing. Maybe we should consider setting a time limit by which, if you don't pay the balance in full, we would have to discuss the option of stopping the treatment, at least until you can pay it off." Yet, as it turned out, without such an ultimatum, but merely through the psychoanalytic work as indicated, she paid up-to-date at the beginning of the fourth year.

Middle Phase

Resolving the debt seemed to open up a greater sense of freedom for her. She imagined that I wished to impregnate her. "I feel like I want to do whatever you want, to please you, but that scares me, it feels so weak." She expressed relief that she was not shoplifting any longer. "It was so stupid, so risky, and it made me feel diminished, less of a person." In the weeks that followed, the patient many times referred to herself as "reviving, like Springtime, or Easter, like the dead arising, like Jesus coming out of the tomb." She elaborated on romantic fantasies about me: "I just have to use a technical term! I guess I'm having a 'positive transference'." I said, "Do you need to use a technical term, to dampen down your feelings and make them feel safer?" She said, "Yes, that's right. I had a pain in my abdomen, then the beginning of my period, and I thought it must have been the pain of ovulation. I thought, maybe I'm re-emerging as fertile, and then I can have your baby." But sex was good for her, she said, only when hatred was involved. She wished to sit in my lap and get me excited, and complained that the frustration as she thought about it made her feel "frantic". She reflected on her tendency to abuse men.

The next week, she said, "I realize something is changing here. I've been amazed that I've been able to tolerate my feelings toward you significantly more. Even hearing your voice makes me feel good. You did that 'leaning forward' thing — to think that you're focused on me, paying attention, and speaking to me, allows me to feel — I guess it's love — oh, that makes me so nervous!" In my countertransference, although of course I never said this, I experienced something similar toward her, an agreeable sense of satisfaction in being with her, in our work together, and in her easier progress in the analysis. This seemed to increase my patience and tolerance. She was letting me come to know and appreciate her intimately as a person in greater depth. I wished to hear and took pleasure in hearing her elaborate her thoughts, and felt this consistent with my therapeutic task as I understood it, of attempting to help her recognize and remove resistances as they arose, so that she could experience and acknowledge derivatives of unconscious conflicts, increasingly undisguised. Occasionally, however, I worried that I was unknowingly letting myself be gratified inadvisably. My erotic feelings and perceptions may have obscured from me the full awareness of her continuing wishes to punish and murder me; I felt no conscious fear, pain, nor humiliation. I also now wonder if I may have communicated this to the patient despite myself. The danger would be that she may have felt reinforced in her fantasy that if she could only win my love, she would be magically cured. On the other hand, many if not most patients involved in psychoanalysis (and analytic therapy) feel encouraged to seek their analyst's love. This may be the natural response to an analyst's proper role and behavior, and, in any case, may be a helpful if not a necessary motivator for progress in the treatment.

Over the following months, we saw that her wish to stay with me forever, that we should grow old together, was one tributary of her maintaining the unrealistically low fee. She became more willing to address the fee in a practical manner. Once we arrived at a higher but still low fee, at the end of the fourth year, she said, "Paying makes this feel more real. . . . Now I feel that the point is to get finished and get out of here. The psychoanalysis is very real emotionally, but in my real life I have nothing, and the years are ticking away. My relationships with men are empty." (Her only sexual relationship was with a married man.)

She worried that her feelings toward me would lead her to "step out of line." There ensued countless elaborations of her admixed love and sadism toward me, threatening her with anxiety, depression, and guilt. In one session, at four and one-half years, she reported a dream in which, "You were sitting on my bed next to me, leaning back, so you were kind of behind me. It was real cozy. I felt so gratified. I could talk and you were interested and would listen, like here, too. It felt wonderfully safe. When I feel that you care about me, it's so exquisitely uncomfortable; the feeling is so sharp, I can't describe it. It's beautiful. . . . Later in the dream, I'm lying in bed and your head is down here (she pats the couch next to her hip), and I'm patting your hair. It was relaxed and okay, but your head, I think, was disembodied, and there was this little line of skin, like a ridge, on your forehead, as if there were a small opening. . . . It felt very affectionate, as if I were holding G (her friend's two-year-old son) on my lap. A wonderful feeling!" [She here hugged her arms across her chest and sighed as if she were holding the boy on her lap.] The next day, she said that the ridge of skin was a penis: "I had beheaded you, in both ways." I asked, "How do you mean?" She answered, "Well, your head and penis were detached. You were—a dick head! Sorry." I asked, "Do you wonder at your need to apologize?" She said, "The odd thing was, it felt so calm and peaceful." I said, "For you." At this she laughed uproariously. "That's right! It felt so— weird. I don't want to go on with this! I went to Sunday school, remember? [laughter] I'd like to see a pastor analyzed, just for the torture of it. . . . But my feelings toward penises have always been awe. I've been abused by penises." I wondered if her sexual ideas, which progressed to further images of my being diminished and humiliated, weren't designed unconsciously to "tie up" me and the psychoanalysis. She wanted me to feel a failure.

Comment:

This could be termed an "undisguised transference dream," in which the analyst appeared as himself. Notice how the dream at first was not bizarre, but almost realistically replicated in some respects the actual situation in the analysis. Her feelings in the dream were of extreme pleasurable gratification at receiving the analyst's close attention. Her consciously aggrandizing him may have served to defend against other wishes, to diminish, weaken and hurt him. Then, the dream became much less realistic. Her loving affection, like hugging a small boy, replaced other feelings that might have accompanied beheading the therapist, and keeping his head by her side: sadistic power and mastery.

Let's focus on the therapist's comment, "For you." On the one hand, it was quite spontaneous, obviously humorous, and ironic. The patient's uproarious laughter probably indicated the effective communication of what had been left implicit: that the beheaded, emasculated state probably would not be so comfortable, calm, and peaceful for the therapist. Without planning, the therapist had entered into what for him during his work was an unaccustomed manner of speech. Perhaps he had unconsciously joined the patient in her own idiom. This had beneficial effects, as the patient evidently did enjoy the sense of naturalness and togetherness between them. On the other hand, he was not being "neutral and objective" in his usual style of reflecting back his observations and conjectures about the meanings of the patient's expressions. Instead, he had evidently been caught up in the affective intensity of the disguised "pleasurable" sadomasochism. His humor in effect joined her defense against recognizing the horror of beheading. We might say that his comment was a "mini-enactment", in which he accepted her use of him. On the other hand, it evidently also served as an effective defense-interpretation, as she immediately saw the implications, that in the dream she was expressing her castrative wishes and pleasurable sadism.

By early in the fifth year, the patient was coming much less late. She seemed to become more free, for example, telling me, "Oh, shut up!" if I made a connection that she found embarrassing. Sexual thoughts about me led her to say, "Somehow, I feel you're making me say these things, but I know you're not." I pointed out that the idea that I was making her would permit her to feel less of a bad person. She said, "They are my thoughts. But if *I'm* having these feelings and doing this, then I have to rethink all the times that I was abused. Was it *me* having those feelings and doing *that* too?" She was getting a new perspective on having been abused and victimized, realizing the possibility that she may have played some active role.

Toward the end of the fifth year, there emerged guilt at how she had been "awful" toward her father; she imagined that she had given him his fatal heart disease. "He was miserable, sick, incapable," she said, to which I pointed out, "Just as you describe yourself." She replied, "Right. I'm just like him, a grumbling person, always complaining and dissatisfied about everything, living an unfulfilled life." I interpreted her identification with her father, her guilt at believing that she had destroyed him. She was enacting a powerful role, treating me as if I were the weak father. She nevertheless had consigned herself to lifelong self-punishment, which I interpreted by saying, "You make yourself miserable like him, denying yourself any nurturance or gratification with a man."

We also explored her need to diminish herself to undo competitive urges with her mother. There seemed (early in the sixth year) to be indications of significant change, in her admitting pride and fondness toward her mother, as we clarified her conflict of having wished to please her parents, at the same time despising them. "I tried all my life to take care of my parents, but it's like my mother didn't want me to have a life of my own. I could never leave; I would get such a guilt trip." I said, "And maybe my bringing up the reduced fee feels like a guilt trip from me, as if I'm saying you shouldn't have a life of your own." She responded, "Right. How can I, when I should be giving you more? But I end up feeling that I'm a burden on you. . . . It must be terrible to be you and have me come here every day."

Comment:

The analyst, for our purposes, obviously is grossly abbreviating the middle phase of this long analysis. Still, note how the patient's working through her past traumata of being sexually molested, and her object relations with the representations of her parents, was interwoven with her working through of the transference. The therapist was sometimes father, sometimes mother.

Negative Therapeutic Reaction Worked Through

Over the next year or so, the patient often took my defense-oriented comments as a reason to disparage herself, and she frequently trivialized what she was talking about. Her attacks on herself, of course, were implicitly attacks on me, punitive and demeaning, if disguised with light humor. For example, she said, "I know that I can control my feelings. The analysis has enhanced my performance in life. But inside my head, I feel worse. My self-contempt has just grown and grown, the longer I come here and think about these things." I noticed to myself the incongruity of her words with her affect, which was buoyant and good humored. She was teasing me sadistically, as when she said, "Everything I find out about myself is bad." I thought this was a protracted negative therapeutic reaction, by which she needed to undo or prevent clinical progress, as an expression of further "negative" transference feelings and conflicts. I interpreted this to her in various ways. For example, I said, "You have to condemn yourself for what we discussed, rather than thinking it's something for us to understand." I also felt that she was wishing to spoil the therapy out of envy of "the good" I had to offer, and I later said, "It's as if there's a competition. If I make you better, I win. If you remain depressed, feeling bad about yourself and your life, then you win." She said, "Right. But where does this get me? I'm just a sick person." I now wondered if her pleasant laughter each session wasn't ironic, as if she were presenting defensively to me a parody of her life. A few weeks later, she was able to acknowledge her need to suffer and enjoy it: "I'm trying not to be depressed, but I want to be. I really like it. It's kind of peaceful." When she said, "I have felt, when my mother dies, that then I can go on with my own life. That's how I feel about the analysis; when this finally ends, then I'll be able to move on." I thought she was in a mother transference, wondering if she could ever extricate herself.

I continued to address her fears of and defenses against intimacy with me, and I pointed out that her not doing positive things for herself may have been an expression of destructive feelings toward me. I would also point out how quickly and persistently she turned away from me, in order not to let herself see her vivid interest in me. She had a dream in which she was with a boy to whom she was very attracted. They were kissing, and "I was very turned on. And then, I think I started to take his shirt off, and there was something about his hair. He had no hair on his chest. It was perfectly smooth, and I got completely turned off. And I thought, 'What am I doing here?' It reminds me of how yesterday, at the end of the session, I had a fleeting thought about your hair. I was thinking, 'When are you going to get a haircut?' You seem to be one of those guys who gets a short hair cut, and then lets it go until your wife says, 'Your hair is getting too long. It's time for you to get a haircut.' That short haircut really does work best for you. But see there? I'm thinking that you're feeling fed up with me, like, what right do I have to tell you about your haircut? I just can't get this right. I feel like I'm very stupid and should just plan on leaving, because what right

do I have to say these things to you? It seems too intimate. I know I'm supposed to have those feelings, but I just don't."

I said, "It's so hard for you to notice how quickly you brush aside any such
feelings about me that start to come up. You don't want to think that there
could be a connection between your being turned off by the man's lack of hair
in the dream, and then your comment to me about my hair." I later said, "Do
you notice how no sooner do you let me know that you've observed something about my person, my hair, that you then feel very anxious, that I must
be fed up with and will reject you?" Later, I said, "You seem very concerned
that it's presumptuous for you to say something wifely to me. As if that's
something you absolutely should not let yourself do."

Comment:

*Again, the therapist, on the one hand, was following his intuitive sense
that the boy in the patient's dream was a disguised "transference allusion." She more or less confirmed this in her being "reminded" of her
thought about the therapist's hair the day before. The therapist immediately picked up on her persisting reflexive need to disavow her "wifely"
interest. He also showed her how, to accomplish that disavowal, she still
at times needed to disable her ability to notice her own mind at work, her
defensive functioning ("But see there? . . .").*

After countless such episodes in our dialogue, she gradually did become able
on her own initiative both to see and to acknowledge transference meanings
in displacements, for example, in thoughts or dreams about other men. She
said, "You and I have this relationship here: it's going on in my head, and it
must be in your head, but it's too real. You're too important to me. You know
me better than anyone else ever has in my life."

We worked extensively on her identification with her father, in relating to
me as the mother. For example, when she complained of her life being "point-
less" again, and how she hated her work, I pointed out, "Just as your father
hated his work." She reflected on how she had felt "compelled to be like my
father, always unhappy and complaining, feeling a failure." This work resulted in considerable lifting of her depression. Becoming to some degree relieved of having to struggle with this father-identification, she now felt it
might be permissible for her to have more freedom than he had had.

Her tone was predominantly calm and reflective, as when she said, "One
thing that's changed in the analysis is, I used to feel so disconnected from
every stage of my life, except the one I was in, but now, I feel connected to
every stage. It feels like me. I feel like the one who has lived my life. . . . One
thing that's gotten so much better through the analysis is that whole thing
about sexual abuse. There are still issues about power and men, but I don't

feel damaged and ashamed now like I did. It doesn't determine who I am."
She referred to the eventual need to terminate, but in an indeterminate fashion: "The thing is" [crying and wiping away tears], "I hadn't realized what a
big thing that will be. While driving home, I was thinking about telling you
things. You're in my mind all the time, as the only person I'm really close to.
So when this ends, I'm scared I'll be really lonely again."

Termination Phase

At the beginning of the seventh year, she was bringing up termination, but not
as if she were planning really to leave. I had until then remained neutral on
the question, looking at her thoughts with her, but I began to worry that by
saying nothing definitive, I may have been inadvertently implying that I was
willing to work with her forever, and thus tacitly may have been standing in
her way. Thus, in context, I did describe the usual way that people agree on a
termination date, discussing the pros and cons together. She said, "Now, I'm
ready to work, and I think it'll take about a year. When I first came here, I had
no idea that I would fall into, I guess you'd have to call it, such a deep resistance. Before, my thoughts of leaving were as a failure and a defeat for
both of us. Now, I'm thinking, 'Why don't you finish what you came here to
do, and get on with your life?'" We agreed on a termination date at the end of
the seventh year.

With about four months remaining before the termination date, she reported a dream: "I think I was married to this man. He was keeping dead bodies in the refrigerator. I think it was a woman, but maybe it was a deer. Because its feet were hoofs, but they looked like high heels. The body was cut
into pieces and all wrapped up. I felt that we were going to get caught." I
asked, "We?" "Me and this guy, by the police. Cause I felt that I'd participated in killing it. That body in the refrigerator was so unsettling. . . . You
know, I can see why I want to terminate. I'm just tired of hearing myself talk.
It's just words that mean nothing!"

I wondered, "Do you say that it means nothing, in order to dismiss the
dream, to not think about how it might be related to what's going on with
you? You did associate immediately to the termination here." I soon pointed
out, "You'd be 'a dear' to me." At this, she laughed: "If I were dead, or if I
leave, maybe then I'll be a dear to you. . . . Maybe I'd be leaving behind parts
of me." I commented, "Leaving behind parts of you that I could keep and preserve?" She went on to worry that she had overstayed her welcome. "If only
I had been good and free-associated, and didn't censor, or act out. It's like I'm
holding onto your pants leg, and crying [imitating a very small child crying]
'Don't leave me!'"

I wondered to myself if my having agreed to the termination may have represented to her my being "fed up" with her. Regressively becoming like a child deflected her from experiencing or recognizing the aggression implied in dismembering a body. She was attempting to "preserve" me, though she still needed to kill me. Also, she herself would be preserved and kept, trapped in the freezer, perhaps an image of her claustrophobic experience of the analysis at this point: She was "frozen", and couldn't get out. She said, "I just don't feel I can do this, finish the analysis off." Yet, until I called it to her attention, something kept her from noticing the murderous connotation of that phrase. She was titillated and satisfied by the images of killing and bodies, and found murdering me entertaining, not grim. Not having yet made the termination date definite and fixed also helped her put off fears that the termination would be bloody. She felt "not ready" and pushed back the termination date three months further.

It seemed at this stage that she had become able more vividly to see and experience her primitive urges and to understand the role that they had played in her life and in her mind. She imagined straddling me in sexual intercourse, choking me to death as my penis broke off inside her. This would resolve her issues about terminating; she could be rid of me while keeping what she wanted from me. "I can bite off a penis if I want to . . . but if you think I have an unfriendly relationship with the penis, it's much worse toward my vagina." The next day, she said, "I still can't believe it's taken me seven years to get to this, and talk about these things. It's like the whole analysis has been leading up to this year."

With about a month to go before the agreed upon termination date, the patient decided to extend the therapy further. "I never got enough, my fair share, of being a baby that was cared for. So maybe I'm concerned that I might wish to cling to you like an appendage." I asked, "Cling to me like an appendage?" She burst out laughing and said, "I didn't say that! I didn't!" I asked, "Is there something very upsetting about what you said?" She replied, "This is why I haven't wanted to think too freely. I'm afraid I'll go crazy, or that I have already. . . ." I said, "You haven't said what that would be, that would make you so much afraid of going crazy." She replied, "Well, I wasn't thinking about anything more than clinging to my mother's skirts, but when you said it—the idea that I would be your penis. I fear that I'll go crazy—couldn't I? . . . I feel really excited. Maybe I can fix this. It's like *you're* the good mother who's letting me be a baby as long as I like. I'm being weaned quickly enough from your appendage." I asked, "That sounds different from being my appendage." She laughed, "I know. I don't want to say it [she covered her face in embarrassment]. The vision of my being attached to your penis with my mouth, like it's a baby bottle, as long as I want, that's what this is, really."

By the middle of the eighth year, not only the patient's consistent punc-
tuality, but also her warmth and bright smile each morning as she entered
the office, seemed to indicate a new quality or dimension to our relationship. She was enjoying the analysis: "It's driving me crazy! The stuff I said
yesterday, about me falling on my knees and begging you to have sex with
me, and then the reverse, that I want you to beg me! I have to tell you about
this dream. I know it's about you and the analysis. For once, I can say this
before I tell you the dream. This man is coming to cut my grass. A professional man. I know it's you. And I suggest to him, 'Aren't you wasting your
talents on this project?' This man—you—was showing me this lawn. He
had cut it very carefully; it was very formal and complex. I felt that that was
a waste of his talents, to do that for me; I wasn't worth it, and it reminds me
of the low fee here, with your having so much training and talent, devoting
all this time to me. Of course, I couldn't do this without the low fee, but was
it worth it? . . . Then, there's this really weird part, where I'm in the house
and the head of President Clinton (she says this laughing) is on the bed.
Maybe the rest of his body was under the bed. He was alive, and I was talking to him! He does have a big head. Now why do I have to consult such an
oracle? Why couldn't I consult the Sphinx? I am such a lowlife slut." I said,
"Do you notice how you have to cut yourself down immediately, right after
cutting down Clinton?" She replied, "It's just like me, to choose a sex-
crazed maniac to consult with." I said, "The one you consult with." She ex-
claimed, "Oh, stop!" and laughed. "Well, of course, I consult with you. Really you are just a big head to me. That's all I have of you, your thoughts.
And even then, I just have your thoughts about me. I don't get to hear what
you think about anything else." Later, as she was having difficulty making
sense of her own thoughts, I said, "Perhaps you keep yourself from connecting your thoughts about the dream, because it would frighten you to be
telling me what it's like to cut off my head and keep it with you on your bed
to consult with." She replied, "Oh, that would be nice! That would be wonderful! It's like I pet and kiss my cat before I go to work, and I really love
it if he's in the exact same spot on the couch when I get back. That would
solve the whole termination thing." I said, "Then you would always have
me, and you'd be the one in control." She agreed.

Comment:

*As the patient herself remarked, it was a sign of analytic progress that she
had learned to interpret her own dreams, especially regarding the previously forbidden feelings, wishes, and urges toward the one actually with her
as she spoke, i.e., the analyst. The attitude of eroticized playfulness and
"fun" almost outshone the fact that she was clinging in her dream still to a
devalued self-image, with major transference implications. ["It was a waste*

of his talents . . . I wasn't worth it."] She seemed at first in the dream to be expressing an admiring, appreciative image of the therapist as skilled and careful in his complex work, of whom she was undeserving. In many ways, she disavowed her sadism against him. It is striking that she should yet again have a dream of beheading the therapist, while the manifest affect is affectionate. As in another just-described previous dream, the body is stored, this time under the bed. The sadistic pleasure, power, and love appear also in her making the therapist her pet, there for her to keep as long as she likes. We might think the dream served defensively to undo the real loss approaching in termination.

As the designated termination date approached, I noticed in myself a countertransference emotion of buoyant excited anticipation, as in the last weeks of preparation for a wedding or a graduation. She dreamt that she met her first boyfriend again: "I really loved him. His family were lovely to me. They adored me. Anyway, in this dream, I was hugging him, and I felt so much love, all the intensity of love I felt at nineteen. I was saying, 'I'm so glad you're back!' And at the same time, I was horrified at the intensity of my feelings. It was scary. . . . In the first weeks of the analysis, I had this wonderful fantasy that I was special to you that way, and I was luxuriating in it. Then, it all got blown away." Yet again, she disavowed the joyful embrace, teasing that all she had gotten out of the treatment was a hundred thousand miles on her car. At the same time, she marveled at the disappearance of a lifelong symptom, her inability to urinate in a public bathroom.

Enactment in the Termination Phase

As we entered the last week, the momentum of new material and insights seemed only to be building, for example with regard to unresolved sexual issues in relation to her own and men's bodies. She had broken off the affair with the married man she had been seeing, and had started dating other men. With days left, she admitted to having cold feet about the planned termination: "How do I know I'm ready? How come I wasn't talking about these things over the past eight years? Why did I have to wait until now?" She worried that I was anxious to be rid of her. She realized how much of an investment she had made in the analysis, and said, "Wow! I really chose this!" She thought perhaps she was an asset to me, "but I don't want to be foolish and overestimate myself. See, as soon as I start to think that you might wish for me to stay, that it would be a loss to you, this harsh voice comes up inside, spitting in my face, and says, 'Yeah, right, don't be an idiot.' I have to immediately, harshly, suppress myself. I'd give anything to understand why that should be necessary." This illustrates how she had been able to internalize reliable automatic self-analytic functioning, to identify with the analytic process.

In the next-to-last session, she began with, "Well, I hope you're satisfied. I was thinking, what if I just refused to leave? I can do that. And what if I refused to raise the fee? I am in control, it feels. What could you do? . . . It's like the power that a child has over the parent. You had me! You're responsible for me! You can't get rid of me!" I said, "I had you." She went on, "Yes, it's been a long labor. Maybe you'll die." She imagined that I had stretch marks from her. "There's no denying that I've had a significant place in your life and in your practice. This is it! You are stuck with me for life. When you're old and retired, you *will* think of me. You can't forget about me. It's been too long, too significant. I don't want to give you up now. Being able to say that I want to have power over you and be inside you: You couldn't have pried that thought from me a few years ago! All those voices whispering, 'Don't say that!'—to hell with them!" [She here made a sweeping gesture with her arm through the air.] "Growing up, you had to be a good girl, which meant keeping such a low profile, you weren't even noticed." I commented, "Like coming late here." She said, "Right! Now I finally have my day in court!" Seizing control and extending the analysis, she seemed elated, triumphant, as if she had overcome some tremendous barrier or opponent; I thought of VE Day.

I felt this was a nearly hypomanic defense against the threat of separation, loss, and grieving, against acknowledging that her wishes were in fact frustrated. Being "inside" me as a baby perhaps defended against other views of what she was doing to me, and, in fantasy, to my body. In retrospect, I notice that I didn't then point out that she wasn't seriously raising the question about whether in fact she could continue. Having seen that I had allowed her to change her mind before, she was presuming my acquiescence. I still wonder how I had placed myself in what may have seemed a comfortable masochistic position, where "whatever she said goes." I, in fact, did consider that some tasks remained unfinished, and that the momentum for yet further significant therapeutic gains was promising. I thought that she saw herself unconsciously both as a man sadistically fucking me, and also as a woman sucking my penis as long as she wanted.

Over the next several months, she at times seemed to fantasize that she was with me because I couldn't get rid of her, that she had enslaved me, not that we had made a rational judgment to delay the termination. At times, she felt "shocked at those things that I have said here about you, that I want your baby. The whole eight years is all coming together now. This feels the most important time of my life. I love you. I just love you. I can't help it." I said, "You feel you should try to stop it?" She went on, "I guess so. It's involuntary . . .

I'm not depressed anymore. I feel confident, open to feeling, and to change. Yet, I feel out on a limb. Like, who am I to love you? What?! Do I think that you might love me? Right! I'm really some kind of worm." I said, "You have to rebound so drastically and quickly from the thought that I might love you." She went on, "Yeah, because it feels so out on a limb. . . . Obviously, my thoughts about you are sexual. I think something really important is happening here: I no longer have sex and love separated. I no longer have the division between a good man who will take care of me and the bad men, the sexual penises of the world." She saw her experience with me as integrating.

Early in the ninth year, it was clear that she also had achieved greater freedom to attend to, explore, and express anger toward me: "This is a sick relationship here. I'm tired of carrying the weight. You don't help me. You're passive and weak. I know this is untrue, but that's how I feel." I pointed out, "You have to say it's untrue, to back away from those angry feelings." The next day, she spoke about weak men and said, laughingly, "I realize this has to do with you. See, I'll save you the trouble of bringing yourself into it." She now made transference interpretations herself. She had a fuller awareness of hating me, of how she kept both of us down. The old pathology was now altered by the dimension superimposed of clear awareness, her ability to observe, and to take distance. She had internalized reliable automatic self-observing and self-reflecting functioning.

She again was asserting her need to go. She struggled with the appeal of staying with me forever. She feared that, if she ended and afterward longed for me, she would feel demeaned. She worried about hurting me if she left, and needing still to repair me. She seemed not to think that everyone has to give up loved ones eventually. She said, "This is the end of the line on that dependency, being like a baby thing. If you couldn't help me get over that. . . ." Sentence by sentence, she still undid her gains, as if she wanted to be sure that I wouldn't stop worrying about her, or feel too pleased with myself. She wondered if a termination date in six weeks would be okay, to which I replied that it would be "not inappropriate." She reflected, "It's demeaning that the analysis was good, and that I have to give it up! It'll be like old love letters in a trunk or attic, I hope. I might forget for a time, but now and then I'll think, 'Now what was it that I knew about this?' And then I'll be able to go to the trunk and pull out the letter. When things go through your brain, it changes the landscape. We've been through all this together, and now, in the forest of my mind, there are these new paths."

Five weeks before the end, she said, "See? Now how did you remember that? And that's why I'll never be able to find someone else who knows me so well. You are uniquely patient and accepting. At least, I can't think of a moment in which you've been impatient with me." I thought later that perhaps this was over-idealization of analysis and of me, and that the ideal of personal perfection may have stimulated her contempt for herself and others for being imperfect, and may have prolonged the analysis. I wondered if she would be able to integrate the sadness of disillusionment.

In the last weeks, she became involved with another man with whom she was excited but frustrated and unfulfilled. Now more consciously, she felt the architect of her own frustration, but she was still angry that this was the best that she could allow herself. I interpreted how with this man, a self-employed alcoholic musician, she was again trying to rehabilitate her father. She felt she had to give it one more try, to make him into someone who would be able to love her, but she said this would be the end of that game also. She recognized that he was hopelessly unavailable. "What, am I crazy? This must really be all about you. I'm acting it out with this guy. You're going back, not just to your family, but to your other patients, to your whole life. I'm at the bottom of the totem pole. I want to hate you. I want to see you as an incompetent screwup, so I can be contemptuous and just go. I feel crazy, because I also know that in recent months, I've said that I feel better now than I ever have. . . . It's not that this relationship is changing; it's *ending*. It's over. It *is* a death." I said, "And it's hard to accept that deaths occur, that loss is normal." She replied, "Right. When my father died, I couldn't grasp the fact that it was absolutely, unequivocally, irreversibly, factually over."

In the next to last week, she happily thought that there might be nothing wrong with her, and she could perhaps have eventually a healthy relationship. "To think it really could be in my heart." "It?" "Self-love. A step beyond someone else loving me." I said, "Maybe it would be scary, because if you left here so healthy, it would mean you really have had an experience here with me so different from what you had with your father."

She said, laughing gently, "That's right. I didn't realize I have been trying to hold onto my father. I always thought that I was trying to let him go. You have loved me. I must be okay. But then I'll have all this love and gratitude toward you. I don't know how I'll deal with that." She experienced tearful grieving that she never got her father to say that he loved her, and now, feeling as if she were on her father's death-bed, desperate, she couldn't get me to tell her how I felt about her.

The third from last day, she said, "I'm just so terrified that I'm not going to have you anymore. . . . Maybe you'll think about me. Maybe you'll jerk off thinking about what I've told you. Isn't that amazing, that I can say this sort of thing? Thursday night in the car with J., feeling simultaneously pity for him, disgusted, and at the same time wanting him to kiss me, and realizing how it all had to do with my father: that's how the analysis came in. That I could see all that together, so clearly, it was amazing, a real brain twist. I'm not panicked. I'm not overwhelmed. I can't leave angry. I can't leave in love with you. I can't see you as perfect. I always wanted to get over these inhibitions, and now I have! I'm tons less inhibited than I was. To have all this mixture: you're not a perfect God, you're not a pathetic failure, and leave it at that. That's what's coming together for me in the past few weeks. There's nothing terribly wrong with me. I am a human being like everybody else. But I get angry that maybe if you had been harder on me, I could have gotten better faster. So I'm grateful and critical at the same time. Years ago, you said something about that, about tolerating opposite feelings at the same time, and something clicked in my mind, but I didn't recognize it happening until now."

Comment:

Again, we can see that, in working through grieving so that she could accept the reality of loss, she at the same time was experiencing the analytic relationship as an avenue for personal integration, by which she was seeing past and present relationships as reflecting one another. She was also realizing that she could tolerate both human imperfection and her own ambivalence; she had integrated deeper appreciation for herself and others as "whole people", both good and bad.

She began the last session with, "Well, here we are—graduation day. Driving here, I thought, maybe I'll just keep driving and spend the rest of my life driving here. It reminded me of that time with my father in the hospital, when I asked my mother, 'What did the doctor say?' and she said, 'I'll tell you when we get home.' I knew what that meant. . . ." She quoted her friends, who said that I must have learned so much from her, and I pointed out how it was important for her to think of me remembering and thinking about her. She said, "Oh yeah, it's critically important. . . . I feel better than I ever have in my life. And you must feel good about that. How could you not feel a sense of pride and accomplishment in what you've done, how you helped me change, making this possible?" She wished for me to say more: "I just want to hear your voice. I want you to put something inside me, that I can take with me." I asked, "Put something inside you?" "Well, you know! I want you in every way. I want your voice inside my head. I want you inside my body. I want your thoughts inside my thoughts. When I was a child, I knew you were out there, somewhere. [She was now choked up.] There was all this evil in the world around me, but somehow I knew there was something better. When I was thinking this, you probably weren't even born yet. But you were out there. So I just had to put my head down and get through the storm that was my life, until I got here. But all the work, effort, and time that we put in has made me better. You put up with all my whining and complaining and lateness. I really wanted you to give up on me and kick me out; I really wanted you to." I asked, "Any thoughts in retrospect why?" She said, "I don't know—it would have proven that all men are bad." She tearfully went on, "The most important thing I want to say is—thank you. I just hope to God that you know how much gratitude I feel toward you. . . . And somehow, I really do believe that you love me. Like maybe you found me attractive at times. And the idea of you jerking off thinking about me—that's fun! It's okay. That idea of sex and love being combined is new. . . . But this is exciting, like a graduation. It's a whole new chapter in my life starting. I'm just fixated on the idea that I'm going to walk out that door and nine years will be finished! Did you ever dream that it would be this long?" As we had to stop, I said at the end, "It has been good working with you." She said, "Oh, thank you for saying that. I appreciate it. It's been—amazing."

AFTERWORD

This analysis illustrates many of the key concepts discussed in earlier chapters of this book. The patient's character traits, insofar as they helped her not to notice potential aggressive or erotic feelings and thoughts, manifested early and throughout the therapeutic relationship as "transference of defense". For example, she made light of herself and of her thoughts and presented herself with much self-disparagement, seeking thereby to limit expectations of herself and to shape the relationship according to previous defensive patterns. One might say that the emergence of the eroticized, idealizing transference also served defensive purposes, for example, in keeping out of awareness feelings of hatred toward and wishes to be destructive to the analyst. Her falling behind thousands of dollars in the fee could be called the re-emergence of an old symptom, "shoplifting", now resulting from and embedded in the process of the analysis itself. This would be one key indicator that a "transference neurosis" had developed, as a "new edition" of her continuing struggles with powerful conflicts that had begun even in childhood.

The transference neurosis not only repeated her early attempts at solution to her conflicts, but also provided access to reawakened memories. The analyst became a central figure in her mental life, representing at different times each of her parents, but also representing at times various aspects of herself. For example, she at times expected him to be aggressively critical and rejecting, as she was toward herself. At other times, she saw him as a weakling she could torture, use, and possess, also a fantasy-aspect of her self-image as a victim of abuse.

This analyst has reported aspects of his subjective experience with the patient, showing how his unconscious may have resonated with hers. The two of them interacted in such a manner as to create a specific and unique therapeutic milieu, difficult to define, but which itself must have had impact on the patient (as well as on the analyst), and thus on the unfolding of the transference. It is clear that the two of them achieved new dimensions of deeper, richer relatedness, the experience of which helped the patient reawaken and realize psychological potentialities that had become frozen. Whether or not the transference neurosis was completely "resolved" through the analytic dialogue, it seems well demonstrated that the patient via the treatment did resume a process of personal development. In the transference experience, she was able to discover and acknowledge intense, previously unconscious motivations, fantasies, urges, and defenses. This unconscious having become conscious, she could then integrate these aspects of her mind into a level of functioning that was more mature. That is, she became better able to relinquish compulsive, depressive, or anxious suffering, and to achieve greater effectiveness, pleasure, self-esteem, and satisfaction in life.

References

Arlow, J. & Brenner, C. (1964). *Psychoanalytic Concepts and the Structural Theory.* New York: International Universities Press.

Aron, L. (1991). The patient's experience of the analyst's subjectivity. *Psychoanalytic Dialogues 1:* 29–51.

——. (1996). *A Meeting of Minds: Mutuality in Psychoanalysis.* Hillsdale, NJ: The Analytic Press.

Atwood, G. & Stolorow, R. (1984). *Structures of Subjectivity: Explorations in Psychoanalytic Phenomenology.* Hillsdale, NJ: The Analytic Press.

Baker, H. & Baker, M. (1987). Heinz Kohut's self psychology: An overview. *The American Journal of Psychiatry 144:* 1–8.

Balint, A. & Balint, M. (1939). On transference and countertransference. *International Journal of Psycho-Analysis 20:* 223–230.

Bellak, L. (1970). The validity and usefulness of the concept of the schizophrenic syndrome. In B. Cancro, ed., *The Schizophrenic Reaction* (pp. 41–58). New York: Brunner/Mazel.

Bellak, L. & Meyers, B. (1975). Ego function assessment and analysability. *International Review of Psychoanalysis 2:* 413–427.

Benjamin, J. (1990). Recognition and destruction: An outline of intersubjectivity. *Psychoanalytic Psychology 7 (Suppl.):* 33–47.

Beres, D. (1956). Ego and the concept of schizophrenia. *The Psychoanalytic Study of the Child 2:* 164–235.

Bibring, E. (1954). Psychoanalysis and the dynamic psychotherapies. *Journal of the American Psychoanalytic Association 2:*745–770.

Bion, W. (1959a). *Experiences in Groups.* New York: Basic Books.

——. (1959b). Attacks on linking. *International Journal of Psycho-Analysis 40:* 308–315.

Brenner, C. (1979). Working alliance, therapeutic alliance, and transference. *Journal of the American Psychoanalytic Association 27 (Suppl):* 137–157.

——. (1982). *The Mind in Conflict.* New York: International Universities Press.

Busch, F. (1999). *Rethinking Clinical Technique.* Northvale, NJ: Jason Aronson, Inc.

Chused, J. (1991). The evocative power of enactments. *Journal of the American Psychoanalytic Association 39:* 615–639.

Fenichel, O. (1941). *Problems of Psychoanalytic Technique.* Albany, NY: Psychoanalytic Quarterly.

Ferenczi, S. (1932). *The Clinical Diary of Sandor Ferenczi.* Cambridge, MA: Harvard University Press.

Fonagy, P. (1991). Thinking about thinking: Some clinical and theoretical considerations in the treatment of a borderline patient. *International Journal of Psycho-Analysis 72:* 639–654.

Fonagy, P., Moran, G., Edgcumbe, R., Kennedy, H., & Target, M. (1993). The role of mental representations and mental processes in therapeutic action. *Psychoanalytic Study of the Child 48:* 9–48.

Freud, A. (1936). *The Ego and the Mechanisms of Defense.* New York: International Universities Press.

Freud, S. (1910). The Future Prospects of Psycho-Analytic Therapy. *Standard Edition, XI*, pp. 144–145.

——. (1912). The Dynamics of Transference. *Standard Edition, XII.*

——. (1912a). Recommendations to Physicians Practicing Psychoanalysis. *Standard Edition, XII.*

——. (1915). Observations on Transference Love. *Standard Edition, XII.*

——. (1917). Introductory Lectures on Psychoanalysis. *Standard Edition, XVI.*

——. (1932). New Introductory Lectures on Psychoanalysis. *Standard Edition, XXII.*

Gabbard, G. (1994). Love and lust in erotic transference. *Journal of the American Psychoanalytic Association 42(2):* 385–403.

——. (1995). Countertransference: The emerging common ground. *International Journal of Psycho-Analysis 76:*475–485.

Gill, M. (1954). Psychoanalysis and exploratory psychotherapy. *Journal of the American Psychoanalytic Association 2:* 771–797.

——. (1979). The analysis of the transference. *Journal of the American Psychoanalytic Association 27 (Suppl. Appendix):* 263–288.

——. (1982). Analysis of transference. Vol. I, *Theory and Technique.* New York: International Universities Press.

Goldstein, W. (1985). *An Introduction to the Borderline Conditions.* Northvale, NJ: Jason Aronson, Inc.

——. (1991). Clarification of projective identification. *American Journal of Psychiatry 148:* 153–161.

——. (1996). *Dynamic Psychotherapy with the Borderline Patient.* Northvale, NJ: Jason Aronson, Inc.

——. (2001). *A Primer for Beginning Psychotherapy. 2nd Ed.* Philadelphia: Taylor & Francis (Brunner-Routledge).

Gray, P. (1994). *The Ego and Analysis of Defense.* Northvale, NJ: Jason Aronson, Inc.

Greenacre, P. (1954). The role of transference: Practical considerations in relation to psychoanalytic therapy. *Journal of the American Psychoanalytic Association 2:* 671–684.

Greenberg, J. (1986). Theoretical models and the analyst's neutrality. *Contemporary Psychoanalysis 22:* 87–106.

——. (2001). The analyst's participation: A new look. *Journal of the American Psychoanalytic Association 49:* 355–381.

Greenberg, J. & Mitchell, S. (1983). *Object Relations in Psychoanalytic Theory.* Cambridge, MA: Harvard University Press.

Greenson, R. (1965). The working alliance and transference neurosis. *Psychoanalytic Quarterly 34:*155–181.

Grotstein, J. (1981). *Splitting and Projective Identification.* New York: Jason Aronson.

Hamilton, N.G. (1988). *Self and Others: Object Relations Theory in Practice.* Northvale, NJ: Jason Aronson.

Heimann, P. (1950). On countertransference. *International Journal of Psycho-Analysis 31:* 81–84.

Hoffman, I. (1983). The patient as interpreter of the analyst's experience. *Contemporary Psychoanalysis 29:* 389–422.

——. (1996). The intimate and ironic authority of the psychoanalyst's presence. *Psychoanalytic Quarterly 65:* 102–136.

Jacobs, T. (1997). Searching for the mind of the analyst. *Journal of the American Psychoanalytic Association 45:* 1035–1059.

Katz, G. (1998). Where the action is: The enacted dimension of analytic process. *Journal of the American Psychoanalytic Association 46:* 1129–1167.

Kernberg, O. (1967). Borderline personality organization. *Journal of the American Psychoanalytic Association 15:* 641–685.

——. (1975). *Borderline Conditions and Pathological Narcissism.* New York: Jason Aronson.

——. (1980). *Internal World and External Reality.* New York: Jason Aronson.

——. (1984). *Severe Personality Disorders.* New Haven: Yale University Press.

——. (1987a). Projection and projective identification: Developmental and clinical aspects. In *Projection, Identification, and Projective Identification,* ed. J. Sandler, pp. 93–115.

——. (1987b). Projection and projective identification: developmental and clinical aspects. *Journal of the American Psychoanalytic Association 35:* 795–819.

——. (1995). *Love Relations, Normality and Pathology.* New Haven: Yale University Press.

Klein, M. (1946). Notes on some schizoid mechanisms. *International Journal of Psycho-Analysis 27:* 99–110.

——. (1952). The origins of transference. *International Journal of Psycho-Analysis 33:* 433–438.

Kohut, H. (1971). *The Analysis of the Self.* New York: International Universities Press.

——. (1977). *The Restoration of the Self.* New York: International Universities Press.

——. (1984). *How Does Analysis Cure?* Chicago: University of Chicago Press.

Lachmann, F. (2000). *Transforming Aggression: Psychotherapy with the Difficult-to-Treat Patient.* Northvale, NJ: Jason Aronson, Inc.

Lichtenberg, J. (1989). *Psychoanalysis and Motivation.* Hillsdale, NJ: Analytic Press.

Lichtenberg, J., Lachmann, F., & Fosshage, J. (1992). *Self and Motivational Systems: Toward a Theory of Psychoanalytic Technique.* Hillsdale, NJ: Analytic Press.

———. (1996). *The Clinical Exchange: Techniques Derived from Self and Motivational Systems.* Hillsdale, NJ: Analytic Press.

Little, M. (1951). Countertransference and the patient's response to it. *International Journal of Psycho-Analysis 32:* 32–40.

Loewald, H. (1975). Psychoanalysis as an art and the fantasy character of the psychoanalytic situation. *Journal of the American Psychoanalytic Association 23:* 277–299.

Loewenstein, R. (1969). Developments in the theory of transference in the last fifty years. *International Journal of Psycho-Analysis 50:* 583–588.

Malin, A. & Grotstein, J. (1966). Projective identification in the therapeutic process. *International Journal of Psycho-Analysis 47:* 26–31.

Meissner, W. (1980). A note on projective identification. *Journal of the American Psychoanalytic Association 28:* 43–67.

———. (1988). *Treatment of Patients in the Borderline Spectrum.* Northvale, NJ: Jason Aronson.

Mitchell, S. (1988). *Relational Concepts in Psychoanalysis: An Integration.* Cambridge, MA: Harvard University Press.

Natterson, J. & Friedman, R. (1995). *A Primer of Clinical Intersubjectivity.* Northvale, NJ: Jason Aronson, Inc.

Ogden, T. (1979). On projective identification. *International Journal of Psycho-Analysis 60:* 357–373.

———. (1982). *Projective Identification and Psychotherapeutic Technique.* New York: Jason Aronson.

———. (1986). *The Matrix of the Mind: Object Relations and the Psychoanalytic Dialogue.* Northvale, NJ: Jason Aronson.

Orr, D.W. (1954). Transference and countertransference: A historical survey. *Journal of the American Psychoanalytic Association 2:* 621–670.

Racker, H. (1957). The meanings and uses of countertransference. *Psychoanalytic Quarterly 26:* 303–357.

———. (1968). *Transference and Countertransference.* New York: International Universities Press.

Ramchandani, D. (1991). Letter to the Editor. *American Journal of Psychiatry 148 (10):* 1409.

Reich, A. (1951). On countertransference. *International Journal of Psycho-Analysis 32:* 25–31.

———. (1960). Further remarks on countertransference. *International Journal of Psycho-Analysis 41:* 389–395.

Renik, O. (1993). Analytic interaction: Conceptualizing technique in the light of the analyst's irreducible subjectivity. *The Psychoanalytic Quarterly 62:* 553–571.

———. (1996). The perils of neutrality. *Psychoanalytic Quarterly 65:* 495–517.

———. (1999). Playing one's cards face up in analysis: An approach to the problem of self disclosure. *Psychoanalytic Quarterly 68:* 521–539.

Rosenfeld, H. (1952). Notes on the psycho-analysis of the superego conflict of an acute schizophrenic patient. *International Journal of Psycho-Analysis 33:* 111–131.

———. (1954). Considerations regarding the psycho-analytic approach to acute and chronic schizophrenia. *International Journal of Psycho-Analysis 35:* 135–140.

Sandler, J. (1976). Countertransference and role responsiveness. *International Review of Psychoanalysis 3(43):* 43–47.

———. (1987). The concept of projective identification. In *Projection, Identification, and Projective Identification*. Madison, CT: International Universities Press, 13–26.

Segal, H. (1964). *Introduction to the Work of Melanie Klein*. New York: Basic Books.

Smith, H. (2000). Countertransference, conflictual listening, and the analytic object relationship. *Journal of the American Psychoanalytic Association 48:* 95–128.

Stern, D. (1985). *The Interpersonal World of the Infant: A View from Psychoanalysis and Developmental Psychology*. New York: Basic Books.

Sterba, R. (1940). The dynamics of the dissolution of the transference resistance. *Psychoanalytic Quarterly 9:* 363–379.

Stolorow, R., Brandschaft, B. & Atwood, G. (1987). *Psychoanalytic Treatment: An intersubjective Approach*. Hillsdale, NJ: Analytic Press.

Stone, L. (1967). The psychoanalytic situation and transference: Postscript to an earlier communication. *Journal of the American Psychoanalytic Association 15:* 3–57.

Stone, M. (1977). The borderline syndrome: Evolution of the term "genetic aspects and prognosis." *American Journal of Psychotherapy 31:* 345.

Strachey, J. (1934). The nature of the therapeutic action of psychoanalysis. *International Journal of Psycho-Analysis 5:* 127–159.

Target, M. & Fonagy, P. (1996). Playing with reality: The development of psychic reality from a theoretical perspective. *International Journal of Psycho-Analysis 77:* 459–474.

Ticho, E. (1970). Differences between psychoanalysis and psychotherapy. *Bulletin of the Menninger Clinic 34:* 128–139.

Winnicott, D.W. (1947). Hate in the countertransference. In *Collected papers*. New York: Basic Books, Inc.

Wolf, E. (1988). *Treating the Self*. New York: Guilford Press.

Zetzel, E. (1956). Current concepts of transference. *International Journal of Psycho-Analysis 37:* 367–376.

Index

About the Authors

William N. Goldstein, M.D., is on the faculty of the Baltimore-Washington Institute for Psychoanalysis, where he is currently director of the Adult Psychotherapy Training Program and has previously served as president of the Society. He is Clinical Professor Psychiatry at the Georgetown University Medical Center, a member of the editorial board of the *American Journal of Psychotherapy* and a reviewer for the *International Journal of Psychoanalysis*. He has recently received one of the Edith Sabshin awards from the American Psychoanalytic Association for teaching of non-psychoanalysts. He has written extensively in professional journals and has previously published four books. Dr. Goldstein currently practices psychotherapy and psychoanalysis in Chevy Chase, Maryland.

A Distinguished Fellow of the American Psychiatric Association, **Samuel T. Goldberg**, M.D., is on the faculties of the Baltimore-Washington Institute for Psychoanalysis and the University of Maryland, School of Medicine, Department of Psychiatry, where he twice has received the Teacher of the Year award. He also has been honored with the Wendell Muncie Award by the Maryland Psychiatric Society. His recent writings have concerned psychoanalytic perspectives on some plays by Shakespeare. Clinically, he consults to a wide range of community mental health settings, and is in the private practice of psychiatry and psychoanalysis in Baltimore and Columbia, Maryland.